WHY
YOU
SHOULD

BUILD YOUR

BUSINESS

NOT YOUR

IT DEPARTMENT

WHY YOU SHOULD

BUILD YOUR
BUSINESS
NOT YOUR
IT DEPARTMENT

**A GUIDE TO SELECTING THE
RIGHT TECHNOLOGY PARTNER**

TO KEEP AHEAD OF THE CHANGES

AFFECTING YOUR GROWING BUSINESS

DAVID E. EISNER

⊐ DATAPRISE

Published by Advantage, Charleston, South Carolina.
Member of Advantage Media Group.

ADVANTAGE is a registered trademark and the Advantage colophon is a trademark of Advantage Media Group, Inc.

Printed in the United States of America.

ISBN: 978-159932-474-6
LCCN: 2015931125

Book design by George Stevens.

This publication is designed to provide accurate and authoritative information in regard to the subject matter covered. It is sold with the understanding that the publisher is not engaged in rendering legal, accounting, or other professional services. If legal advice or other expert assistance is required, the services of a competent professional person should be sought.

Dataprise, Support365 and Cloud365 are registered trademarks of Dataprise, Inc. All other trademarks mentioned or displayed are property of their respective owners.

 Advantage Media Group is proud to be a part of the Tree Neutral® program. Tree Neutral offsets the number of trees consumed in the production and printing of this book by taking proactive steps such as planting trees in direct proportion to the number of trees used to print books. To learn more about Tree Neutral, please visit **www.treeneutral.com**. To learn more about Advantage's commitment to being a responsible steward of the environment, please visit **www.advantagefamily.com/green**

Advantage Media Group is a publisher of business, self-improvement, and professional development books and online learning. We help entrepreneurs, business leaders, and professionals share their Stories, Passion, and Knowledge to help others Learn & Grow. Do you have a manuscript or book idea that you would like us to consider for publishing? Please visit **advantagefamily.com** or call **1.866.775.1696.**

To Nancy: technology is my passion, but you are my love.

ABOUT THE AUTHOR

David E. Eisner founded Dataprise (www.dataprise.com), a Washington, D.C. area-based technology provider, in 1995 and has led its growth from a tiny start-up to recognized leader in providing managed IT services to small and medium-sized businesses. Today, Dataprise has grown to over 200 employees and supports the IT needs for almost 1,000 customers throughout the Mid-Atlantic as well as nationally. In 2014, Dataprise was recognized as one of the top 15 managed services providers (MSPs) globally by *MSPMentor*. An Ernst & Young Entrepreneur of the Year Award® recipient, Mr. Eisner was recently honored with the Tech Council of Maryland's Executive of the Year award as well as being named to the MSPMentor 250 Top People in Managed Services.

Mr. Eisner holds both a bachelor's and master's degree in computer science from the University of Maryland and The Johns Hopkins University, respectively. He is an alumnus of the Entrepreneurs' Organization and the Board of Visitors for the College of Computer, Mathematical, and Natural Sciences at the University of Maryland.

Mr. Eisner and his wife, Nancy, live just outside Washington, D.C. in suburban Maryland. They have a daughter, Nicole, and twin boys, Dylan and Alexander.

WHO SHOULD READ THIS BOOK

This book is for those responsible for evaluating, purchasing, and selecting the information technology needs of small to medium-sized businesses (those generally with less than 250 employees). You own or operate a business or manage its IT functions. To understand the concepts discussed in this book, you do not need any specific technical skill sets, but you should be generally aware of how modern office technology can affect your business and employees. You should keep an open mind about changing paradigms in technology and support. Put simply, if you are accountable for the technology needs of your business, this book is for you.

This is your guidebook on how to choose an IT partner and navigate technology in the 21st century. I will show you pitfalls to beware and opportunities to pursue. To compete in the new millennium—locally, nationally, globally—all businesses need to do things faster, smarter, more efficiently. Technology gives you the means to do that.

TABLE OF CONTENTS

INTRODUCTION

WHEN THINGS CHANGED FOREVER

My parents bought me my first computer in 1979, when I was 13. It was a now-vintage Apple II, and, at the time, it was quite an expense for my family, a couple thousand dollars. I was hooked from the moment I first booted it up.

It had only uppercase keys. For a monitor, I used an old black and white television, and it stored the programs I wrote on a cassette recorder. I taught myself how to program using Apple BASIC. At first I used this marvelous machine to organize and graph my middle school homework, which I'm sure reassured my parents that it was worth the price. Soon I was writing simple games (and playing them, too).

Back in the early 1980s, I didn't have to worry about how to connect that computer to other high-tech devices. Even if I'd had other devices, there was generally no means of connection other than a really slow dial-up modem. And there was no Internet.

Life and technology were simpler then. Things were about to change forever.

●

Whether you are a start-up or an established business, you cannot survive and grow in this day and age without essential information technology (IT)—the computers, PCs, laptops, mobile devices, tablets, and more. So many questions: How much of what do I need to buy? How do I get it all connected together? And even if I can get it to work, how will it help me?

In our modern world, you most likely know, at a minimum, how to browse the Internet, write an email, and print a document. If you have grown up in the last 20 years you have learned to use technology as a critical tool for school at a very early age. And if you are in the workforce today, undoubtedly technology plays a major role in just about every aspect of your work day.

Have you ever stopped to think about all the things that are necessary to keep that technology working smoothly? From your device, to the network, to the Internet and back again there are dozens if not hundreds of connections and applications that all most work together harmoniously. Today we've just come to expect that like the car in the driveway, our technology will just be there when we turn it on.

Ask yourself how long can you go without access to your email or ability to connect to the Internet? An hour? A day? A week? These tools have become the lifeblood of our entertainment, education, and business lives.

I bet most people probably can figure out how to hook up the cables and wires and connect some of the devices that they use every day. And many folks know how to connect to the Internet "cloud" and how to download and run a myriad of the ever increasing quantity of mobile "apps".

Beyond that, most need a professional's guidance. And that's where people like me come in. I've been in the technology business and specifically the technology management industry for more than 20 years. It's what I do: "tech support" (among other things). I've been lucky enough to take my long held passion for computers and leverage that into my own business of supporting other business information technology needs and challenges.

One of the things I've discovered in building my own business, Dataprise, is that a small business owner would rather focus on what they do best, which is running and growing the business—providing that service, making those widgets. Businesspeople aren't tech people, for the most part. They know they need IT tools, but they would rather just listen to one source of good advice.

Why won't IT just fix itself?

Despite what you may have seen in a movie or read in a book, technology doesn't generally self-assemble or repair itself. It has, however, gotten smarter. Many computer operating systems can now automatically download the latest software patches automatically, and popular software programs can also install the latest updates behind the scenes, all without human intervention. This means that the total cost of ownership (TCO) for installing, building, and maintaining business technology has decreased dramatically in the last decade, and that's great news for business owners and operators who can now leverage the same technology tools as their largest competitors. Just don't look for your PC's hardware and software to (1) run forever without an issue, (2) fix itself completely when something does go wrong, and (3) understand how to work harmoniously with systems connected to itself, by itself. At least, not anytime soon. ⬡

In the last 10 to 20 years, it has become unmistakably clear that technology can be used to accelerate and grow any size business. Once you understand that, then the next question must be: Where do I go for help?

There are so many different choices today in business IT, so many ever changing pieces to the puzzle—mobility, the cloud, a wide array of PCs and servers and devices and software. How do you make it all work together? It can feel mind-boggling, even for people in the IT field.

Most businesses today need some way to crunch and sort and collate an avalanche of information. "Big Data" and "business intelligence" are the new frontiers. We have the ability to catalog and analyze millions of tidbits about what people are doing, what they're reading, which websites they're visiting, and what they are doing there. If you are opening a flower shop, for example, you can map the thousands of other flower shops across the country, find out what they're selling, and learn about their customers.

You can do all that from your armchair, using a PC or tablet connected to the Internet. Understanding how to do that and what tools to use is important if you want to get ahead of your competition. Most entrepreneurs want one-stop shopping—and this book will help you identify exactly what you need and where to find it. My goal here is to take a load off your mind. You don't want to worry about technology. You want to work on growing the business.

THE RIGHT TOOLS, THE RIGHT PARTNER

I understand how puzzling the onslaught of technology can be. Many of today's businesspeople started out with a standalone PC or even a typewriter. They have seen a torrent of technological change that continues to this day. They saw the parade of photo-copiers and fax machines and PCs and laptops and smartphones. They've progressed from dial-up to Wi-Fi and beyond. That's just a fraction of what they have had to deal with.

Some technologies come and go, but the Internet certainly is here to stay, and we'll be dealing with its myriad of security issues and threats for the foreseeable future. Certainly it seems likely that businesses will be harvesting Big Data increasingly in the years ahead, as well. We will be computing and telecommuting and reaping the benefits of the technological age.

The premise of this book is to provide small business owners with the right tools to select an IT partner to help them grow. You will learn about a variety of alternatives that will help you decide what's right for you as you strive to keep ahead of the changing technology.

This book is not a tutorial on the fast-changing technologies available today or coming tomorrow, but rather, it is about how to get aligned with a partner who can keep track of and manage it all for you. You need someone with experience in staying ahead of the game.

Regardless of the technology du jour, what is important is how to wade through a morass of technology solutions and choices and find someone who can assist you. It is very similar to aligning yourself with a good doctor, lawyer, or accountant. Such professionals are responsible for staying abreast of their particular expertise, and we rely on them to do so.

We likewise should rely on a professional in technology. You need a partner, just as you would for financial, legal, and medical

Where are the geeks?

A big misconception in the technology business today is that if you want a challenging computer problem fixed properly you need only summon a bespectacled computer "geek" from the nearest computer store and throw them at the issue.

Perhaps that is the right approach if you are faced with a minor technical glitch or configuration issue such as trying to connect a PC to a device like a document scanner.

But when it comes to supporting one of my business clients, being a geek means you've had significant professional technical training and certifications, you can communicate proficiently, and that you have the necessary people skills to support the most challenging business environments. As a small business IT purchaser, you should make sure that "professional" goes hand-in-hand with "geek" when evaluating your business IT needs.

By the way, if you talk to my wife or one of my three kids they will surely say you need look no further than me to see a shining example of a true "professional geek." Hopefully, they mean that as a compliment. ⬢

advice. That has not always been obvious, and yet it is critically important. Men and women of business cannot know it all. They may be experts on their product or service, but they are not experts in technology—and why would they want to be?

Most of the big IT manufacturers over the last 10 or 15 years have tried to make consumers and business owners believe in do-it-yourself (DIY) technology, using phrases like "plug and play" and "quick start." The industry wants to make everything seem simple so that you are encouraged to buy.

But any small business owner who has purchased and unpacked a complicated server, or tried to get a wireless router to install, has seen how complex the technology can be. Sure, a particular device or software may not be all that complicated to use, but making it work cooperatively with the rest of the technological world is another story. That, again, is why you need to pick a partner who can stay ahead of this for you.

Time is money for the modern businessperson. You lose money by spending your time fiddling with technology. It is generally not the best use of your talents and resources. You wouldn't try to be your own lawyer or your own accountant, so why be your own IT guy? You could be making a lot more money doing the things you do well.

THIS THING CALLED PERSONAL COMPUTING

I still have that old Apple II in my basement, and it still works perfectly. It reminds me of my early curiosity about how and why things work—the fundamental questions upon which technological change has always been based.

When I was a kid, I would take apart my toys, particularly the electronic gadgets and radio-controlled cars. I'd get a birthday gift, and within a day I'd be attacking it with a screwdriver. I had to know what made it tick. Then I'd try to put it back together—with varying degrees of success, much to my parents' dismay. It is that kind of curiosity, I believe, that leads a lot of people to technological careers.

In terms of technology, the late 1970s and early 1980s were primitive years compared with today. Kids used pocket calculators which were considered high technology. Not only was there no Internet accessible to the general public, but there was little in the way of productive software. Word processors and spreadsheets were just starting to come out, and 1981 saw the birth of the PC era.

Those early computers were introduced to homes way before they became commonplace in the office. They often ended up as dead weight; when the child got bored of using it, it would gather dust. That wasn't the case in my house. I wanted to figure out what my computer could do. It came with some toy software but didn't have much applied purpose. I had this tool, but what was I going to do with it? How was I going to apply it? And so, I learned to graph my math homework.

I always tried to learn the next thing. I played and I tinkered. I had plenty of time to explore, it seemed—a luxury that too many kids lack today—and I wanted to learn the insides and the outsides of this new thing called personal computing.

That interest stayed with me through high school and at the University of Maryland, and it has stayed with me throughout my career. In some ways, I'm still doing the same thing now that I was doing when I was 13 years old. I am essentially still figuring out how to apply this thing called computing and helping others do the same.

Small business owners face the question every day: How do I apply technology to solve the problems that I'm facing in my bakery, or my flower shop, or my law firm, or my accounting firm? I help others learn to apply the technology around them in the most efficient way for their businesses.

CHAPTER 1

EYEWITNESS TO CHANGE

had no computer in my dorm room at the University of Maryland during my freshman year in 1984. Back then, if you wanted to log on to the computer, you'd have to go to the library and stand in line. Personal access to technology hadn't come a long way yet, but it was raring to go.

In my postvinyl but predigital college days, my music collection was mostly on cassettes: Foreigner, Journey, Genesis, the Who—and of course the Beatles and the Stones, who endure through the ages. I'd slip a cassette into my Sony Walkman and drive off in my souped-up maroon '81 Olds Cutlass Supreme. Life was good.

And life was also about to change, dramatically and forever.

I had gone off to college with a desire to study technology. Back in that day, when kids like me leaned toward technology and were comfortable around a computer, the guidance counselors tended to suggest that they study engineering in college. So that's what I did, for a few years.

I failed miserably—at first. Engineering was just not for me. It was hard-core physics and chemistry. It was fluids and dynamics and mechanics and circuits. It had nothing to do with what I had learned on my Apple II computer. I found myself foundering— until, during my junior year, I took a FORTRAN programming class and aced it. I had found the field for me.

My advisor suggested that I take a relatively new track at the University of Maryland called computer science—the study of how to use computers to solve problems. I switched majors from engineering and worked hard to earn a computer science degree. Later I went on to get my master's in computer science from Johns Hopkins University. I'd found a field of study that suited my interest. Once I found that, I excelled.

A RELIABLE ADVISOR

I see that experience as another example of how you have to apply the right solution to the right challenge. I wasn't meant to be a mechanical engineer. I was trying to get my degree by using the wrong tool with the wrong application. Changing to the right tool and the right application made all the difference—and for me, that application was computer science.

Each of us has a place, a niche, a skill set. I respect engineers. They excel in their specialty, but many of them know little about computer science. They, too, need IT people. Nobody can play every role in life, or in business.

Majoring in computer science changed everything for me by providing the passion that allowed me to succeed. From high school my goal had been a technical degree, and as I entered college

I wasn't able to distinguish the difference in alternative paths to getting that degree. It wasn't until I looked much closer that I saw that one path led to failure and another to the right solution.

That's how it is for businesses that are looking at technology solutions. It is not until you get down to the details that you see the stark differences. That's where you need good advice. In college, I finally got the advice I needed from a good advisor.

Business owners need good advisors, too. If they make the wrong choice about the tech track they should take—as I made a wrong choice in college—they could waste valuable time and resources. Most of us can think of a time when we made the wrong choice and paid the consequences. Even as you are reading this, you could be making the wrong choice on managing your technology.

A FRONT ROW SEAT ON CHANGING TECHNOLOGY

While I was in college, I interned for a start-up software maker and later at IBM, which became my first real IT job.

Before that, however, I had worked part time during the summers in the back office of a tiny clothing retailer and in the account department of a small pharmaceutical company. I input data onto spreadsheets. That experience showed me that small businesses, just like big ones, needed a technology infrastructure.

* In the late 1980s, small business technology was a whisper of what it is today. There was no ubiquitous Internet. Only the largest or wealthiest of companies could afford an office network

or LAN, and there were really no shared resources. The decade of the networked PC didn't come until the 1990s.

The 1980s was the decade of the standalone PC, with a printer directly attached. The office may have shared a fax machine, but the networking technology was in its infancy. Shared business resources and collaboration tools like email were virtually nonexistent. Small business software like networked accounting systems, databases, and applications were only starting to be developed. Web sites didn't exist.

Files and documents and floppy disks were moved by "sneakernet," meaning you hoofed them to their destination. That was the long and the short of how most small businesses were interconnected circa 1990. Later in the mid-90s, local area networks, or LANs, became very popular, and business owners began to understand how they could benefit from not having to go across the hall or across town to share data and files. The sneakernet died as local networking and ultimately the Internet grew. Businesses could see what they *could* do, although they didn't see it as what they *must* do.

In the two and a half decades since my college days, I have been fortunate enough to see most of the evolution of the modern era of the IT field firsthand. I've had a front row seat on all the changes. And I'm happy to report what is now obvious: the IT field has evolved, and come into its own, as a necessary part of doing business.

Technology is a big enabler and mover for any sized business. It changes industries, people, jobs, careers, and lives. It has slammed the newspaper industry hard, for example—although if newspapers are dying, many will go to heaven and live again online.

Consider that Amazon founder and CEO Jeff Bezos recently purchased the venerable Washington Post for $250 million. The evolution of the traditional and the technological is evident in the deal.

The fate of many traditional print outlets is a cautionary tale, and another reason why small business owners need to pay attention. Technology is the only facet of their enterprise that can either put them out of business or vault them ahead, depending on how it is used or not used. Those in a small or growing business who don't pay attention to technology trends do so at their own risk.

Small businesses need to be thinking first and foremost about the partners they utilize. In my view, that's the big decision—not which technology to choose but which partner can best help to leverage technology. Unless you go to school and dedicate a tremendous amount of resources and time, you'll never be an expert on all the comings and goings, facets, features, advantages, and disadvantages of different technologies. You could do that no more readily than you could keep up with medical advances and surgical techniques.

I have seen a change in the nature of how businesses perceive technology. I'm no longer educating them on the why. I'm educating them on what's next. In 20 years of running my business, I have seen a big change in customer perspective. Once, technology was a supplement, something nice to have. Now, technological efficiency is absolutely mandatory for survival.

AN EVOLUTION OF UNDERSTANDING

Today I talk to so many small business owners who are just starting to get it. It's like musical chairs. The music stops and they scramble to hook up with a good IT partner.

It wasn't that way when I was getting out of college and starting my business. Small business owners didn't seem to want to hear anything about getting a technology partner. In the mid- to late 1990s, they often still wondered why in the world they would need a business email account or an onramp onto the Internet. They had a lot to learn—but in the years since, many of them have learned it well, at least so far as understanding the need for such technology.

In those early years of my fledgling IT consulting business, when I first began talking to other small business owners about how I could help them, I was mainly educating. I would sit down with the owner of XYZ Company, and the conversation would go something like this:

> Me: "You know, you can get an Internet circuit that you can share with your 10 employees."
>
> Owner: "We don't need to share the Internet. See, we have 10 modems and 10 dial-up accounts. What more could we use?"
>
> Me: "With shared Internet, you can get your own domain name for your whole business. You can call it xyz.com. And everyone can have an @xyz.com email address."

Owner: "Why would we need that? We have 10 employees, and we share an AOL account. Besides, we don't get much email."

Me: "If we networked your PCs together, you could share files and use just one or two printers."

Owner: "Each of my employees has their own printer."

Most of my time then was spent educating business owners on what they could do and why it would be beneficial to do it.

I would talk about the burgeoning Internet. "Did you know you can now hook up all your PCs in a network?" I would ask them. "And that those PCs can share an Internet connection so that all your employees can browse the web?"

"Why would we want them to do that?" the business owners often would exclaim.

So then I would talk about how employees might dial in to the office from home to access files and work documents over a modem. Or use a single shared printer.

I knew by the mid-1990s that business email was going to change everything. But I talked to many people in the small business world who didn't believe that. Sure, they had an email account, maybe with AOL or Erols, but it was just one address that they expected to serve the entire company. If customers needed to reach the company, that's the address they would use.

I tried to convince them to establish a domain name for the business. That not only would give the firm a corporate identity on the growing Internet, but each employee could have an individual email address. They had a hard time seeing why that mattered.

Today, the value is undeniably clear—and as email morphs into group texting, we are speeding up interpersonal communication a thousandfold to customers, partners, employees, and colleagues.

Technology is about scaling. It provides solutions to help businesses of any size compete on a national and global scale. Email, websites, the Internet, blogs, and social media are tools of scale. These tools are great equalizers in a global market. You can have a hundred conversations in an hour, vs. the one or two you might have over the phone.

But back in 1995, many failed to see that potential. They had a new race car at their disposal, and they wanted to power it with a rubber band. And this was true even for larger small businesses. Just before I started my own company in 1995, I was working for a technology defense contractor just outside Washington, D.C. with a little over 1,000 employees. The company had just installed a dedicated Internet circuit restricted for use by a small select group of its top executives. Regular employees like me weren't assigned an Internet email address. Internet email had technically been around since the mid-1970s, but it didn't catch on as a priority until the mid-1990s.

Now, fast forward 20 years. We're no longer having to explain to a small business owner why they need the technology, why they need to have connectivity and email, and shared resources, and security. Now, when the music stops, everyone jumps for a seat at the table with a good partner. The question is no longer about whether they need technology. It's about which technology they need—and how to keep it running.

LAUNCHING MY BUSINESS

I was 28 and had very little money saved in 1995 when I started Dataprise. I was no entrepreneur or nouveau business maverick. I simply hated my job.

I was paying off my student loans, living in a small apartment with three roommates like a lot of young single people. I had been working a few years in the industry as a programmer for that government contractor (perhaps you have seen someone like me in that movie Office Space?). It was at the very beginning of the dot-com boom. The Internet was exploding onto the scene.

Some of my friends were making big dollars writing software for fledgling web firms, start-ups flush with venture capital. I didn't know any rich venture capitalists or start-up companies. I did have other friends who had quit their jobs to become independent consultants in the IT field, meaning they hung their own shingle and went out with a suit and tie and keyboard trying to make money by giving expert advice on technology.

When my employer announced that the company was going to be sold, I knew it was time to make that leap, too, and take the risk. Being broke and single, with little to lose, I looked for my own independent consulting opportunity.

I quit my job March 14, 1995. I started Dataprise on March 15. I had been working on setting up the concept for a few months, on weekends and after hours. I had no clients or money, and so I scrambled to get work and stay busy.

I had good experience as a software engineer and systems designer and programmer by that time, so I tried to see if I could get a few clients to listen to me. They didn't. No one wanted to hire a 28-year-old without a lot of practical experience to advise them. I had worked with government agencies, banks, financial institutions, and larger technology companies in my capacity with my now previous employer, but no one would take that chance with me independently.

I did get the ear, however, of some very small business owners who had really no other choice. I knocked on doors and got referrals in the Washington area. I became the free advice guy. I would hook up with someone in a small business and peddle my expertise.

My pitch was basically this: "Look, try me out for free. I will give you some free tech advice and I will educate you about the Internet, and networking, and Microsoft Windows." I would donate my time, because that's all I had. I got a reputation as a guy who would show up when called.

Slowly, I won people over. I grew a small but loyal group of customers who could count on me to give them good and economically sound advice about their own technology and where IT was headed. Eventually, I was able to convince about a half dozen customers to pay me a few dollars for a few hours of work.

"Thank you," I told them, "but wouldn't it be really nice if I could do this for you regularly and be there for you whenever you have a problem?" That was my introduction to recurring revenue. I was able to create a continuing relationship.

That became my business goal—to regularly sell really high level technology advice to small businesses. I established my niche in helping small business owners to embrace, leverage, and maintain their technology. That was the premise for my business in 1995, and that is what I am still doing today.

A MANAGED SERVICE PIONEER

Today, Dataprise has over 200 employees and supports almost 1,000 growing organizations of all types and sizes—the vast majority being small businesses, which I define as having 10 to 250 employees. We focus primarily on that small business segment.

Dataprise was one of the first to provide what today is called "IT managed services." I worked on a monthly retainer. Most independent consultants would sell their time. They would work an hour, bill an hour, working for time and the cost of materials. That's tried and true.

But when I first started my business, one of my customers told me: "If you could package this in a way that made sense, I would buy it and I'm sure other business owners would too." So I created what I called my bronze, gold, and platinum IT support plans.

I would offer, at different rates, packages of hours provided monthly, 4 hours, 8 hours, or 10 hours. The cost per hour was cheaper for a platinum plan than for a bronze plan. And I added some additional features like rapid on-site response, preventive software updates, and remote telephone support. Purchasing one of my IT support plans meant I would be there on a regular schedule and offer support for PCs, servers, and just about any other business technology. Offering a bundled IT service plan was a novel concept 20 years ago. It was simple to purchase and understand.

I was one of the first people, certainly in the Mid-Atlantic or Washington, D.C. area, to offer a prepackaged IT support plan. We created that and put it on our website. Within about a year, I had sold about 30 of them. That model, in a modernized form, is largely what we do today, and the industry seems to have adopted it. Not long after I began mine, I started seeing such plans springing up all over the country.

I don't know if I was the first, but I was one of the first.

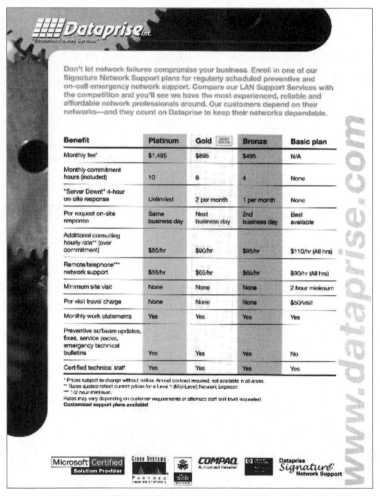

Benefit	Platinum	Gold	Bronze	Basic plan
Monthly fee*	$1,495	$895	$495	N/A
Monthly commitment hours (included)	10	8	4	None
"Server Down!" 4-hour on-site response	Unlimited	2 per month	1 per month	None
Per request on-site response	Same business day	Next business day	2nd business day	Best available
Additional consulting hourly rate** (over commitment)	$85/hr	$90/hr	$95/hr	$110/hr (All hrs)
Remote/telephone*** network support	$55/hr	$65/hr	$65/hr	$90/hr (All hrs)
Minimum site visit	None	None	None	2 hour minimum
Per visit travel charge	None	None	None	$50/visit
Monthly work statements	Yes	Yes	Yes	Yes
Preventive software updates, fixes, service packs, emergency technical bulletins	Yes	Yes	Yes	No
Certified technical staff	Yes	Yes	Yes	Yes

* Prices subject to change without notice. Annual contract required, not available in all areas.
** Rates quoted reflect current prices for a Level 1 (Mid-Level) Network Engineer.
*** 1/2-hour minimum.
Rates may vary depending on customer requirements or alternate staff skill level requested.
Customized support plans available!

Don't let network failures compromise your business. Enroll in one of our Signature Network Support plans for regularly scheduled preventive and on-call emergency network support. Compare our LAN Support Services with the competition and you'll see we have the most experienced, reliable and affordable network professionals around. Our customers depend on their networks—and they count on Dataprise to keep their networks dependable.

A dawning of managed IT support: Dataprise Signature Network Support plans circa 1999

From the beginning, what I have hoped to do has been to show small business owners a better way. I've been watching the direction of technology since I was a 13-year-old unpacking that Apple II. I've been on the front lines for decades.

The technology likely will be very different just a few years after I write this in late 2014. But this isn't a book about today's technology. Even if you are reading this many years from now and are considering innovations that aren't even on the horizon today, my point is the same: Smart business owners need to delegate the management of technology to someone who will serve in their best interest.

AN AFFINITY FOR SMALL BUSINESS

My emphasis remains small business to this day because I understand how it feels to be snubbed by the big guys. Many years ago when no large corporation would take a chance on a young guy without chops, it was the small businesses that put their trust in me. They, too, had been snubbed by the large manufacturers and consulting firms, and so they turned to me.

Twenty years later, small businesses still often feel snubbed, and today a service niche has grown up to support them. Dataprise has been doing that from the beginning. I understand that small business owners often are embroiled in a struggle to survive in today's market. They must stay ahead of the competition, and leveraging technology allows them to do that.

I feel privileged to be able to offer what I know about technology to help others survive, and there's no better customer for me than a growing business. Small businesses have been largely overlooked by big business and big IT manufacturers and big IT consulting firms, and they've had nowhere to go. That's the way I felt when I started Dataprise, and the big businesses, with their own IT departments and big consulting firms, turned me away. Small businesses came to see my value to them. We are a natural fit. We're two outsiders, in that way.

Now the landscape has changed and people are paying attention to small businesses. In the last five years in particular, everyone is jockeying for a piece of the small business market, which is the fastest growing aspect of our economy. It creates the most jobs. And so two decades after the Internet began to boom, there are many IT support options available.

So many choices, so little time. As if the technology alone weren't enough to boggle small business owners, now they have a variety of IT management options to choose from. First, there were too many technology choices and nowhere to go. Now, there are too many places to go.

These are life-and-death business decisions. The penalty can be severe if you make the wrong choice with the wrong technology and invest in the wrong application, the wrong accounting system, the wrong membership system, the wrong website partner, the wrong IT marketing company, the wrong networking technology. You lose your data. You get infected by a virus that you can't kill. Your security is breached. Most importantly, you fall behind.

The reward for choosing well, however, can be unprecedented growth. This is not something that is a nicety or optional anymore. At bare minimum, small business owners are seeing technology choices as essential if they are to function. They are seeking to hook up with the right partner and purchase the right assets, software, and training. They recognize that is how they will beat the competition.

THE CRITICAL QUESTIONS

If you are reading this, you are probably a business without an internal IT department and with a limited budget and resources. You understand what technology can do but lack a depth of expertise. You have some level of localized technology installed at your office. It may include a website, and it certainly includes your networking equipment and your printers. You're running Office applications like Word and Excel. And most likely you've taken at least some initial steps toward entering into this new thing called cloud computing, and you probably want to learn more.

Most likely today, you have somebody who is responsible for helping you manage and maintain the technology—a volunteer, an employee who knows something about technology, or an occasional consultant. Perhaps you have chosen a technology provider to help you on a retained basis.

Those are the most likely options that you have today. It is very rare nowadays to find a company that has no technology support at all, either internally or externally, where it is all left to the business owner. Simply put, if you are moderately successful and have been running your business for a while, you're going to have some technology infrastructure. You will have a website, email, and some mobile devices. And you will have someone who is responsible for maintaining those.

If that description fits you, these are the critical questions: Are you getting all you can get from that person or provider? Are they giving you direction? Are you getting your questions answered, and is their advice taking your business in the right direction?

There are technology providers out there that specialize in specific industries and professions. They may do a good job addressing issues involving your niche, but they may not have broad expertise to help you in other areas.

In terms of market segments, we're horizontally focused at Dataprise, meaning we support businesses in many diverse industries. We tackle the challenges that every business faces with the infrastructure of PCs and computers and resources. We make sure applications stay running. We deal with security, website, and mobility issues that are common to just about every type of business.

Good advice is the key to leveraging IT for a small business. You want to spend limited resources wisely while staying on top of the latest trends and techniques, which sometimes change daily, and receiving top-notch support to keep the technology going.

People and technology need to work together seamlessly. Technology should constructively disrupt the way we work and think about tasks, productivity, and efficiency. It should never be a burden or a money pit.

Most small businesses, while recognizing the importance of staying abreast of technology, cannot afford a dedicated IT department staffed by expensive professionals day and night—and the good news is that today a business doesn't need one. This is especially important in a down economy. As businesses have scaled back on number of employees, they have found that they need to depend on their technology infrastructure all the more.

They need guidance to leverage that technology. They need somebody to show them what is best for their particular needs. In finding that assistance, they need to understand clearly their options for IT management.

As an eyewitness and participant in much of the technological change that has transformed business and society, I am pleased to be your guide.

CHAPTER 2

IT's THE LIFEBLOOD OF YOUR BUSINESS

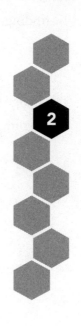

"We could always depend on our typewriters," my newest client told me, not long after I started Dataprise back in 1995. "Now we have to worry about *these* things, and they're so slow," he said, gesturing toward a roomful of desks, each with a PC atop it.

The businessman, who ran a highly successful property management firm, told me that the new hardware broke a lot, and the vendors updated the application software a few times a year, which was both costly and complicated to handle. The software also was full of defects or bugs, and when the computers would freeze or crash, which they often did, the only solution was to call in the computer consultant to do upgrades, install patches, and sometimes switch out spare parts.

"We just can't keep them up and running," he said. "Who needs this grief? We were doing fine, and now we have to rely on these things."

I did what I could to show him how to reduce his expenses while helping make his systems more reliable. Eventually the firm was able to interconnect its PCs so that they operated as a network, and eventually my client became a little less nostalgic for the typewriter.

It was not uncommon in those early days to meet clients like that, who were wistful for the old days even if they understood that the change was inevitable. The complaints came mainly from what we call the "late adopters," or those least inclined to spend money on new or the latest technology.

FROM NOVELTY TO NECESSITY

It was the big business people, the government, education, and universities that were more likely to spend money and try new technologies out. The small business folks didn't generally have the resources to throw around. They saw new technology as a luxury. As long as they could, they clung to their mechanical adding machines and analog phones and typewriters and photocopiers and fax machines. That seemed enough.

IBM introduced the personal computer (PC) in 1981. When the PC hit the business market it should have flopped. It was expensive, came with almost no useable application software, was terribly slow, and wouldn't connect to any other PC. A small business might have purchased one for the accounting department and attempted to run fledgling spreadsheet software. But most folks would stand around the green phosphorous screen and try to figure out what to do with it.

But, slowly, businesspeople began to use it. They had been used to their typewriters and carbon paper. Now they tapped out a few business letters on the basic word processor and printed them out on a dot matrix or a Selectric typewriter-style printer. They tried their hand at some spreadsheets.

By the mid-1980s, the PC and a myriad of PC clones had moved from novelty to necessity, although technology was still quite a stretch from becoming the lifeblood for small business that it is today.

In 1995, at my new firm Dataprise, we experienced that same evolution of technology in our office. Being a technology advocate from the outset, I'd always try to stay a little bit ahead of the curve. We'd always buy the latest computers and technologies and software applications. We were early on the Internet with a four-page website.

Even so, our early days as an office were archaic by modern standards. We didn't have a fast Internet connection or anything like it. We had multiple fax machines. We had a standard multi-line phone.

And we had about five printers—for an office of 10 people. Twenty years later, we have more than 200 employees, but we still have only about five printers. Those days of having a printer for each person are long gone.

There was certainly a discovery period in the mid-1990s where everyone was trying to figure out how PCs, local area networking, and especially the new Internet would benefit them the most. That's when we saw the explosion of LANs as they connected more office workers to one another and to the Internet. We'd left behind the days of sneakernet and peer-to-peer networking (connecting two computers directly together), and we'd stopped carrying floppy disks around. We could just copy files to a shared network server, and even email them. That change laid the foundation for so many of the other advances in small business technology.

Our office, like everyone else, walked before we ran. At first we had these islands of technology, isolated silos of PC, printer, fax machine, modem. In time, we replaced that with the burgeoning network technologies that we ultimately recommended to our clients. Just as importantly, over time we became faster and more efficient at performing many of the pre-Internet tasks. And soon, we learned to depend on them.

TECHNOLOGY AS THE GREAT BUSINESS EQUALIZER

In the past, it had always been the human resources that business considered most crucial to their operation. If you had a problem to solve, you'd throw more people at it, and that would work in almost any situation for any kind of business. Technology started to change that formula. You wouldn't necessarily have to add more overhead and more people—and more expense—to solve a small business problem.

Technology is what I call the great business equalizer. It allows a small business to compete like a big business side by side in today's market. It allows a struggling business to rely less on the human factor or labor to do manual, repetitive tasks. Technology,

With "Tech" comes "Tech Support"

Technology can be the great business equalizer, but only if it continuously works right. This has been true since the beginning of the Industrial Revolution and more recently since the post-World War II era ushered in traditional office equipment such as the electric typewriter, paper copier, and fax machine. IT is no different. As businesses depend more on technology, they invariably depend more on the systems and people who support it.

if used correctly, can be the best friend your business will ever have. Technology can enable even a small mom and pop operation to compete not just locally but also globally.

The train has left the station on whether technology is here to stay. Nobody doubts that technology provides a good return on investment. But technology is like the stock market in that you have to invest to make money. The question is where to put your resources and what to invest in and finding the right advisor. Technology is a bedrock asset to any business if leveraged correctly.

The challenge now has become which technologies to use, how to get good advice, and putting those technologies to best use. By doing that wisely, a small business can compete shoulder to shoulder with big ones. Once, if you were small business located in Washington, D.C., you might never have an opportunity to sell to customers in Chicago, Los Angeles, Houston, Atlanta, or Miami. But now, with the prolific growth of the Internet, any business without bricks and mortar locations across the country can compete with multinational companies.

The travel industry, for example, traditionally has been a local or regionalized type of business. Prior to the mid-1990s, there were thousands of small travel agents, either independent or affiliated with larger companies. Agents were in virtually every hometown. If you needed a vacation, you would visit or call your local travel agent, who would have connections to all the airlines and different vacation packages.

The agents arranged travel for businesses, as well.

In the mid-1990s, along came web-based travel sites like Expedia and Travelocity. With attractive websites and easy to use technologies, they effectively superseded the travel agents, Users could connect directly to the pricing of many different airlines and make instant bookings, bypassing the agent. Those two companies became a powerhouse virtually overnight. Travel quickly became a do-it-yourself operation.

In some ways the explosion of technology hurt traditional small businesses, moms and pops, and independents. If you stand still and you don't embrace technology in today's marketplace and you don't do it quickly and smartly, you're apt to be retired or outpaced by other businesses in your industry that are using technology to their advantage.

It's not something that you can ignore. If you don't evolve your business to leverage technology, you can rest assured that your competitors will. Those local travel agents went out of business unless they stopped selling the old bricks and mortar way and connected to nationwide providers like Travelocity and Expedia.

In the late 1990s, one of my early clients was a relatively large Mid-Atlantic based travel agency with at least half a dozen offices and probably 100 employees. When I found that client, it was already in financial trouble and under pressure from the new Internet-based economy. We tried to help the agency to modernize with networking technologies, optimizing their existing investments. While we were able to help them save costs and become more efficient, ultimately they made the critical error of not advancing their own business model and adapting to the new dot-com reality, and they eventually went out of business.

The lesson to be learned from this is twofold. First, you need to embrace the right technological approach for your business. Second, you need to leverage the right technology to support that approach. Standing still in this technology-enabled world is fatal to a business. Technology can be your best friend, but if you aren't careful, the friend can become the enemy.

TRANSFORMING SOCIETY

In 1994, Jeff Bezos created his website Amazon.com and overnight was able to change retailing to compete with every small-town bricks and mortar bookstore nationwide.

You could search for products. You could price them. And you could buy them with a simple-to-use shopping cart mechanism, and almost magically your purchases would appear in a few days shipped right to your doorstep or office. Bezos had created an integrated supply chain that would connect to a variety of major distributors, and he put distributors directly in touch with others—all through a clever website. He made a little bit of profit on the sales, and the rest is history. Amazon advanced from just books in its first three or four years to include a huge variety of online retailing.

Amazon was an example of the mid-1990s technology boom that changed everything, seemingly overnight. The Internet had changed everything. People were banking and buying online. They were exchanging messages. They were browsing for information and reading online all for the first time. Those who didn't accept it were destined to be left in the dust. Though the Internet has its roots in a government DARPA-sponsored project of the early 1970s, it was not until the mid-1990s that it became so prolific that basically every individual and every business had to have access to it to be successful. Although those connections were laborious at first—many folks can remember dialing up their AOL or EarthLink accounts—certainly the Internet enabled much of the fast-paced growth in the 1990s.

By the mid-1990s many small businesses were realizing two things. They saw that IT could help them transform and project themselves so they could have the advantages of a much larger corporation. And they realized the consequences if they didn't change.

But there was more. The pace of technology was increasing at an almost exponential rate. Hardware manufacturers such as Dell, HP, and Cisco made huge advances in processing power, storage space, and speed. Telco carriers such as Verizon and WorldCom were churning out faster and faster pipes to the Internet. And software manufacturers such as Microsoft were making similar advances in their software applications and network operating systems.

The Internet and these technologies didn't just transform businesses. They transformed society. Anyone who remembers lugging boxes of record albums between their home and their dorm can attest to one way our world has changed forever. The music collection that once made a shelf sag will now fit on a tiny chip. We went from vinyl to CDs to digital downloads, which began in the mid-1990s as well. The digital age has dramatically affected almost every industry.

EMAIL: THE FIRST "KILLER APP"

Do you remember your first personal business email address? Most people do. Email for business changed everything. With email messaging, distributors in California could communicate with their suppliers in Japan. Employees in New York could send documents to employees in Washington, D.C. All almost instantaneously. And just as quickly, the pace of business and productivity overall accelerated.

Email allows a business to magnify its presence and reach all corners of the globe. It helps a business of any size compete because email broadcasts information to recipients at a speed and more importantly a volume that is similar to the largest of businesses, even governments. But business email is more than just a medium. Along with a website, it is the beacon of a corporation's identity. Email ushered in the dot-com era, and to this day a business will often spend significant amounts of money for the most appealing "you@yourbiz.com" types of Internet domain addresses.

No single software application has transformed business and probably society as a whole more than email—the first truly universal critical business application. By the mid-1990s, the rise of corporate email saw the welding of information technology to business at a speed and manner that had never occurred before. Email—including the tools and systems to support it—became a bedrock of business and business technology.

HARD TIMES, NEW PERSPECTIVES

It's clear, then, that the modern era for small business technology began in the mid-1990s. That era rushed in all the modern amenities—email, word processing, websites, networking, and the paperless office—that we've come to take for granted today, not just in business but in our personal lives.

Over the next decade, those changes took hold and grew. Then the Great Recession of 2009 gripped the economy—and once again, attitudes changed. Until then, many businesspeople still were unsure of just how important technology had become to their business. In the United States, unemployment was in double digits nationwide. Businesses of all types were struggling, whether they were aligned with technology or not. "What is it going to take to save us?" they were asking—and once again, technology came to the rescue.

As the recession took hold and the economy remained stagnant, we were very busy at Dataprise, contrary to what many businesses in other industries were experiencing. The reason was that companies of all sizes, and small businesses in particular, were no longer able to make investments in new technology. In other words, they were not going to purchase new equipment, and they were not going to upgrade their servers and PCs.

In fact, many businesses affected by the slowing business climate were forced to lay off employees. Some closed altogether. People were worried that the recession would become another depression.

Even so, businesses understood that while perhaps they couldn't spend money on new technologies, their survival depended on maintaining and supporting the technology invest-ment that they already had made. It was more important than ever that the systems, software, and technology all work together smoothly. If a company's HR department went from three people to one, if its accounting department went from five to two, it needed to bridge that gap with well-functioning technology—more software, better applications, whatever it took to gain productivity. Small businesses turned to companies like Dataprise for help.

After the recession eased in 2010, a new perspective seemed to predominate in the small business world. Technology was not only here to stay, but it was the lifeblood of small business operations. And that lifeblood required expert support and advice to keep flowing. Until then, many had considered uninterrupted email to be a luxury. If a business had no email access for a few hours or a day, it would survive. If your website crashed, you could just wait for the next day. If you lost access to voicemail or to your files, you would be okay. And texting still seemed to be something that just the kids were doing.

After the 2009 economic crisis, we found that our customers didn't feel they would be able to survive for an hour without these things. The Great Recession had underscored the urgency of overcoming the competition and making the most of technological resources in doing so. IT for small business had become a matter of survival.

We'd already had one major wake-up call regarding our dependence on technology. After the terrorist attacks of 9/11, the cellular infrastructure in New York City and parts of Washington, D.C. couldn't handle the flood of mobile phone calls and text message traffic as people tried to reach out to loved ones. While many understand that a cell tower can handle only a limited number of calls at a time, it took a crisis to show people just how dependent on technology we all had become. I was in Washington, D.C., and we were trying to reach some of our employees who were working at the Pentagon. We couldn't get in touch with them for many hours and thankfully they were among the lucky ones that terrible day. One of the lessons learned from 9/11 is that it showed the nation that we needed ever better technology if we were to effectively communicate in an emergency. The Great Recession sent a similar message to the business world.

We have seen how small businesses have changed in their perception of technology. A novelty became a luxury and then a necessity.

IDENTIFYING PRIORITIES

"We understand that technology is here to stay and that it can help our business," a lot of people have told me. "But exactly how can it help us run our business? What are the most critical aspects to support and manage?" They are telling me, in other words, that they are convinced that they need to invest in technology—but they want to know what is most important and how they will maintain it.

To anyone considering where to invest in new technology, I begin with some basics. There are several common IT functions that virtually every small business should address. First, you want to invest in a website that is not just an online brochure or a couple of static pages. There are many ways to dynamically leverage your website to help drive business and communicate with your customers. Examples include online order taking and providing support, service feedback, and client account status to your customers from your business website.

I've already mentioned email as a universal critical application for almost every business. It's important that every organization has a handle on the core messaging systems it will use to communicate both internally with employees and externally with partners, customers, and the rest of the world. And today there are even more ways to communicate than simply through standard email. Examples include instant messaging, email-telephony integration, and user presence awareness, among other modern features.

Another way to leverage IT is to identify your one thing—your business's own "killer app"—that is fundamental to driving your business. Almost every organization that I've ever seen can point to one critical system or application that is the cornerstone of how it does business. It can be as simple as a specially tailored accounting system to manage all your finances. It can be a customized membership management system if you're an association. It can be a secure legal document manager if you're a law firm. It can be a production fabrication system if you're a manufacturer. Whatever it is, discovering how to leverage your own killer app can help you beat your competition.

Another area to consider is mobility—the ability for your workforce to work from anywhere, whether telecommuting, connecting remotely while traveling, or from home. Any employee should be able to access files and messages and emails 24 hours per day from anywhere.

There are numerous other ways to leverage technology, but those are just a few examples of what we recommend you consider right from the gate.

Then once you understand that technology can be your best friend, you may start thinking about how to rely on this friend more and more: How do I make sure it's always by my side, that it won't let me down, that we'll support each other?

But none of your IT priorities or investments will matter much if they don't work together properly. Traditionally, the concept of technical support is simply the repairing and fixing of issues that arise on a PC or a server or a network. Today, though, businesses need more than that. They need strategy and advice. Strategy provides the direction for a business to leverage its assets in a more meaningful way. Small business owners today get it. They have bought technology and plan to buy more. Now, they want the details on how best to support it. They're looking for the big picture.

THE FOUR PRIMARY MANAGEMENT CHALLENGES

We've found that most businesses, no matter what industry, must deal with four "buckets" of IT management challenges. Following is a synopsis of those challenges, and you will be reading much more about them in the chapters to come.

STRATEGIC CONSULTING

Everyone needs advice, whether legal, financial, or medical—or technological. Strategic consulting is at the top of the IT food chain. It's where the big decisions are made on where to spend on technology and what it can do for a business over the long haul. It looks at where one's industry is headed and how to leverage technology to outmatch and outpace the competition.

In other words, if you're a local bookstore and your competitors are selling books online, you need to figure out a way to sell your books online, too, and do it better.

Technology can be leveraged at all levels of your organization, from your HR to your sales and marketing to your operations, and even to how you communicate with your customers. Getting strategic advice regularly, say quarterly or semiannually, is critical.

The IT landscape is like a buffet. There are so many choices, and knowing what to choose and where to spend your limited budget becomes the critical decision with IT strategy.

INFRASTRUCTURE MANAGEMENT

This is where the rubber hits the road. Infrastructure management is the basic support and maintenance that is required to keep your systems—such as PCs, mobile devices, servers, and software—up and running in the most optimal way.

This is the equivalent of a checkup by your doctor or an oil change by your mechanic. It isn't about deciding which kind of car is best for you or where you are going to drive it. It is about keeping your car running and tuning it up in the event that you want to take it somewhere.

END-USER ISSUE SUPPORT AND ISSUE RESPONSE

When the employees—the "end users"—have a problem, they need to be able to quickly contact a qualified team of experts and get competent answers and results.

Most people today are familiar with the traditional concept of calling the IT help desk (or service desk) when a problem arises.

When employees have a question, they need to be able to reach out to their technology consultant or a team of experts.

This is like switching on your GPS and getting help with where you need to go—not so much in finding the direction but in getting around a roadblock or taking a detour.

CLOUD-BASED TOOLS

Small businesses now must deal with the advent of cloud-based tools and technologies. There are now a great variety of Internet applications and mobile apps designed to assist businesses with common everyday tasks. Examples of cloud-based tools include remote backup systems, online storage, antivirus software, and remote control software. These are typically third party systems that companies can "rent," as opposed to buying or building one themselves. Deciding which cloud-based tools to use to help automate the business is the fourth "bucket" of IT support challenges.

What is cloud computing?

Cloud computing leverages remote applications accessed over the Internet to provide IT resources like servers, email, file storage, etc. directly to end-users no matter where they are located. These systems are usually "rented" to employees that need them meaning that there is generally no infrastructure to purchase, build, or maintain. Cloud computing is a great example of a technology equalizer and today the "cloud" should be a cornerstone of any business's IT strategy.

Those four challenges are the crux of what small and growing businesses today are facing as they consider the ever-widening array of technology management and support choices. What is the overall strategy on how the business will use technology? How will the business support and maintain the technology? Who will it call if something goes wrong or an issue arises—and when will that help be available? And what kinds of technology might the business "rent" from the cloud rather than purchase and own?

In the search for solutions, those are the questions that must be answered. The fundamental challenge is how to deliver a support strategy and a suite of technology tools to a small business that really does not know what it needs—and, worse, what it does not need.

CHAPTER 3

LEAVE THE TEETH PULLING TO YOUR DENTIST

ver the last 20-odd years, technology has become integrated and intertwined with all aspects of business. And no business segment has been more positively affected than small businesses, particularly those with under 250 employees. The information technology era has brought great opportunity to small businesses, allowing them to compete globally. To do so, the technology must operate as a seamless ecosystem. Unless it all works together, it can all fall apart. And with so many options available today, it's hard to know where to start.

So how do you turn a jungle of technologies, systems, and choices into a coherent IT strategy for your business? You need to find an expert. Or better yet, a team of experts. Sure, you could try to learn it and do it yourself. There is no shortage of DIY options available. From coding your own websites, purchasing your own cloud-based servers, configuring your own office Wi-Fi, to using an Internet-based remote data backup system, you can point and click your way through a "buffet" of technology products and services and assemble your own IT infrastructure, often right from your desktop. And DIY solutions are often great for start-ups and the smaller range of small businesses. For example, I often recommend a cloud-based data recovery system such as Mozy Pro data backup for an organization with fewer than 10 employees and not that much critical data. Mozy offers a simple online backup tool that's great for either one or perhaps a few PCs. But for larger groups of networked PCs and servers with large data sets, a fully managed data backup solution is recommended. Moreover, going it alone is not for everyone and the complexities of technology grow exponentially as the size and needs of a business increase.

Think about it this way: you could also try to be your own accountant, or you could yank out your aching tooth with a pair of pliers. You might end up with more of a mess on your hands, though. Some things become increasingly painful if not done right—and IT is one of them.

So the good news is that technology is getting more capable, cheaper to run, and easier to buy. But it can be more complicated than ever to maintain and fix—especially when more people, disparate systems, and applications need to interconnect and work together seamlessly. This is an important point. Even though a single tool or an application by itself might seem simple enough to manage, getting it to work with other systems seamlessly can be a significant challenge.

For example, we've already discussed how corporate email is the ubiquitous "killer app." Every business uses it to communicate. Today, email is the tip of an interconnected system of applications and data. It generally connects to your calendar, tasks, and contacts. You can call up that calendar on your mobile device or phone to check on your appointments. Then you can use that phone to run applications and browse the Internet. On the Internet, you can access cloud-based software such as databases, where you can store your customers' information. That customer information can help you make business decisions and influence how you provide services to your customers. Then you communicate to those customers about those services—using email. The cycle runs from email to email with a multitude of technology and applications in between.

With technology being so fundamental to business operations, it must be kept running, and any trouble in any link of the chain must be addressed. An email system outage will affect everything else that we have just talked about. You can't connect to your calendar. Your calendar can't connect to the mobile device, so you cannot see your appointments. You are basically frozen. Consider your running car. Even if left to idle for a long time it will run out of gas. The oil will become dirty and the filters will clog. Eventually—without routine maintenance and replenishment—the engine will stop.

In the earlier days of email, when it was growing and maturing, you had a lot of alternatives if the email system failed. You could pick up a phone, send traditional "snail mail," send a fax, or communicate on a conference line. You can still do those things, of course, but email is now intertwined with many other functions, and they, too, can cease to work when email is down. You can't set the calendar, communicate effectively with customers, or arrange conferences—and ultimately it affects your ability to make rapid business decisions.

That is why you can't look at your business IT one-dimensionally anymore—as just isolated systems, software, and tools. IT is now multidimensional and interrelated. That is the real benefit of technology's maturation. But that integration can also be an Achilles heel.

THE RISK OF A BROKEN LINK

You can have problems at any link in the information technology chain. There are cross connections just like the joints in a bridge, each with different costs and requirements and challenges and different methods to support them. If email fails, you talk to your cloud-based email provider. If you have a problem with your mobile device, you talk to your carrier, like Verizon, AT&T, or T-Mobile. If you have a database problem, you talk to your database administrator or whoever hosts or runs that software.

It becomes very challenging for a layperson or a businessperson to try to keep track of all those moving parts and make sure they are working together. When the technology toolset is working together well, it can provide a tremendous efficiency boost for almost any business. However, if one of those links breaks, the consequences can be costly and time consuming. With interconnected technology, when one thing stops everything tends to stop, in a domino effect.

One of the primary goals of information technology in business is *integration*—meaning that it all works harmoniously together, seamlessly and behind the scenes, so that you do not have to worry about it. More importantly, a tightly integrated technology system provides the highest level of efficiency to a business. Think back to your car. When the parts of the engine all work together well, you get more horsepower. But because of the increased complexity in any interconnected system, when there is a problem it has a tendency to be very apparent almost immediately—and the impact can often be far reaching.

I often ask business owners, "How long can you be productive without email, or the Internet, or mobile phones, or online calendars?" They generally answer that the resulting break in productivity would be immediate and potentially disastrous. While technology clearly can boost productivity and speed, our dependence on it increases with every IT investment we make. Like our morning coffee, IT can be hard to live without once it is part of our routine.

Think of the fly-by-wire system that is commonplace today on modern jet airplanes. In recent years, fly-by-wire has revolutionized the aircraft industry by automating a commercial aircraft to a point where it can literally fly itself, all by computer. Gone are the old mechanical pulleys, cables, and linkages that pilots controlled from the cockpit. Most people would agree that fly-by-wire systems are significantly more efficient than the old ways, and safer too. But any problems with the fly-by-wire system on an airplane can be severe, because of the dependency on interconnected computers. Similarly, when your business's integrated technologies do not work, a solution can be costly and time consuming. You have got to get it right the first time and work to keep getting it right day in and day out.

Even a decade ago, things were very different, and a generation ago it was almost inconceivable that we would be interconnected this way. Businesses now clearly see the need for this. They have long since given up thinking that they can do without it.

Consumers have come to rely on this amazing app-induced environment, where a mobile phone is used for far more than talking. You use phone apps today for running, for monitoring blood pressure, for checking news, for logging into your bank, for getting boarding passes for an airline, and so forth. Imagine taking a trip and not being able to use Yelp to find a restaurant or not having Google Maps to navigate your way. Your phone has become a focal point for travel. Many people are getting rid of their traditional landlines, especially in cities. Often, a smartphone is the only device that millennials have, such is their dependence on that technology. Businesses, too, whose workforce relies on these technologies, can be dead in the water if these seemingly simple devices don't work.

Again, the Great Recession of 2009 cemented the need for competent outsourced IT support for small businesses. You have to keep what you have running, and you can't do without it, particularly in a down economy. In an up economy, smoothly functioning technology helps you to forge ahead and beat the competition, but in a down economy **your reliance on business IT can be a matter of survival**. A break in the technology chain could lead to your demise. Small companies especially, dependent on their integrated technology, must keep it all working together.

HEADS IN THE CLOUDS

Today, if you are starting a small business, there are many ways to leverage technology completely outside of a traditional office environment. As you start your business, you can rent software cheaply from the cloud. You can rent an accounting system from a company like Intuit, with their QuickBooks or QuickBase online. You don't have to buy anything. You can go to Google.com and run Google Apps to get word processing and spreadsheet software, costing almost nothing. You can go to Microsoft Office 365 and leverage their popular Office applica-tions such as Word, Excel, PowerPoint, and Outlook, and their online collaboration applications such as Share-Point. You can use Microsoft's cloud-based OneDrive to store and share files among your peers. Dropbox and Box.com are other examples of file-shar-ing systems. There are a ton of options out there, many of them either free or very low cost.

You can actually start a business today that is "born in the cloud" and have virtually no internal infrastructure whatso-ever. For micro-businesses, this is becoming a real alternative. If you have fewer than 20 employees,

Thinking of starting a new business today?

Many new small businesses are now "born in the cloud." Here are some suggestions of popular freeware or "cheapware" Internet sites to get you started:

1. Microsoft Office 365 (Office, email, calendars, SharePoint, file storage): www.dataprise.com/office365/ office365signup

2. Google Apps for Business (email, file storage, calendars): www.google.com/enterprise/apps/ business/

3. Box.com (online cloud storage): www.box.com/

4. QuickBooks Online (cloud-based accounting software): quickbooks.intuit.com/online/

5. 1&1 (websites): www.1and1.com/

6. Insightly (sales and contact tracking): www.insightly.com/

and you are in different locations, there is generally no reason you need anything besides a laptop, or in some cases just a tablet device, to communicate and run your email, run applications, and access your resources and files, all online. As a business owner, you can rent all that (often for free). That is a great solution for smaller businesses.

It is very efficient and inexpensive. Small businesses can say, "Hey, I don't need anyone to manage all that." A small business can set up shop quickly, on a shoestring or for free, up to a point.

It is not a big stretch or that complex for someone to set up these things—just go to the websites, make a few clicks, and provision these resources. You slap your credit card down if you need to, and you are up and running with these high-powered online DIY resources very quickly. That's a good solution for a micro-business or start-up.

As the business matures and gets more complex, so will your technology needs. You will start to find that all these cloud systems do not work together very well. Ultimately, every business today that starts to grow and has more challenges will need infrastructure. In the IT world, infrastructure for a small business basically means buying desktop computers, networking equipment, firewall equipment, mobile devices, and printers—all the trappings of a traditional technology office. The more people and resources you have, the more infrastructure you need. You have to keep it running and working together.

The "Do-It-Yourself" Technology Barrier

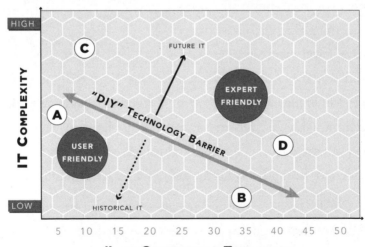

The DIY Technology Barrier shows how the challenges of supporting technology by yourself as the number of networked users and overall complexity increases. In the User Friendly Zone, Area (A) represents medium complexity and a lower number of users which lends itself to DIY support. Similarly, Area (B) represents more users but low system complexity and is therefore also in the DIY User Friendly Zone. In the Expert Friendly Zone, Area (C) indicates a small number of users but high system complexity and likewise Area (D) represents medium complexity and a large number of users. Both areas (C) and (D) represent sufficient challenges to the lay person or someone not sufficiently skilled in technology.

Are we heading toward a day when IT will all be in the cloud? I think it is too early to tell. As long as there are different "clouds" provided by different companies, they will not ever all communicate together seamlessly, and a business will always need some level of investment in its own infrastructure just to be able to leverage the cloud in the first place. So regardless of how much of our future computing ultimately winds up in the cloud, there will always be some required technical infrastructure located locally in the office.

But make no mistake, cloud technology is fascinating and extremely promising, although today it's still in its infancy. At this time, going cloud exclusively can benefit only the smallest of businesses. For most businesses today, the answer is still in the middle—leveraging the cloud when they can, and minimizing investments and saving dollars where they don't need to buy. Renting is always better than buying, and that is one of the cloud's biggest benefits. A drawback is that we have a variety of different clouds and they don't get along all that well. Small businesses can handle some of those inconsistencies and inefficiencies by supplementing cloud systems with traditional technologies.

Salesforce.com, for example, is a great cloud-based CRM, or customer relationship management system. It is used by many large and small companies alike to handle lead and opportunity tracking for sales forces. It is a great system with special solutions to serve a variety of industries such as nonprofits, manufacturing, and accounting, and you can tailor it any way you need. A lot of people use Salesforce.

On the other side, there are numerous accounting systems, such as Great Plains, Sage, and QuickBooks. Those systems have a lot of the same or similar data sets. If you are tracking an opportunity in Salesforce, how do you get the details of that opportunity into your QuickBooks accounting system? This is an example of the challenge of systems that don't necessarily talk to each other.

MAKING SENSE OF IT ALL

When you find yourself with too many choices and not enough deep understanding of the toolsets involved, you somehow have to find your way to a solution. Which tools do you choose? How do you support all this, and how do you make sure it works?

If you still think you can do it yourself, consider Moore's law. Moore's law says the speed of computing doubles approximately every 18 months. With increases in computer processor speeds also comes a plethora of advances in related software and hardware systems. These changes are happening often on a quarterly and sometimes a monthly basis. You can try to learn it yourself, but do you really feel qualified? Is learning how to implement and support technology more important than learning which ones to ultimately use for your business? Again, you might as well be your own mechanic, accountant, lawyer, and doctor.

Every technology that's installed at a business ultimately needs to be managed and supported. If you neglect your health, you'll pay a price down the road. If you never go to the dentist and ignore oral hygiene, you first will get bad breath, leading to cavities, an aching jaw, and ultimately a toothless grin. Likewise, those who neglect their investments in technology will ultimately pay a high price in repairs, downtime, security breaches, and other failures.

It's still a jungle out there. The landscape and the trees have changed, but dangers still lurk. These remain highly complex technologies. Yes, many programs have become easier and easier for people to use, but that does not mean it is easier for people to run an interconnected system. There is a difference.

TO BUILD OR TO OUTSOURCE

If your company has more than about 250 employees, the challenges of scale may call for you to invest in building your own dedicated IT department, likely staffed full time and on-site. At Dataprise, we have numerous larger clients with several hundred employees or more (they mostly use us to co-manage or supplement their own IT department staff), but we generally focus on smaller businesses, for which the much better choice is to outsource. Business IT outsourcing has become a mainstream solution for small business and has grown significantly in the last

10 or 15 years and most dramatically since the financial crash of 2009.

That unofficial dividing line of 250 employees likely will continue rising as outsourcing becomes easier to understand and more affordable—and as companies realize that they can divest themselves of their own IT departments. As for micro-businesses with fewer than 10 employees, they lend themselves much more clearly to cloud-only technologies, requiring almost no infrastructure, that can generally run on a shoestring budget.

Today, I still see many small business owners and managers trying to create and run their own IT departments—or at least attempt to hire their own in-house IT professional. However, this can be a daunting, challenging, and extremely expensive undertaking. When asked, I always say, why not outsource and let the professionals do what they do best?

Despite obvious obstacles, some small businesses feel they can handle the complexity if they just hire "my own guy" to stay on-site and deal with the technology on a full-time basis. Often people tell me that they feel more comfortable knowing their "IT guy is just down the hall." Or they may feel they will have no problem in moving to the cloud. If one of those describes you, and you are not convinced that outsourcing is the right solution for your growing business, there are a couple of things you need to consider.

FINDING QUALIFIED, AFFORDABLE STAFF

Probably the biggest difficulty in creating an IT department—for any size business—is finding the right people. This is very challenging even for IT companies, and at Dataprise we are constantly searching for great talent. In fact, we have a dedicated in-house technical recruiting team to do just that, round the clock. For most businesses, recruiting people with serious technical skill sets is just too difficult. First, how do you know what to look for? Do you understand all the nuances of an IT resume? There are a lot of different skill sets out there. Do you need a network architect, a systems engineer, an operating systems guru, a cloud consultant, or perhaps a security expert? What technology certifications should this person have? What academic background? What experience level? The list goes on and on. The challenge of what to look for in this person is very complex for the uninitiated.

Another consideration is whether you can afford this person. A qualified senior network engineer or a systems manager can easily demand a package of over $100,000, all-in with salary, benefits, and training. It becomes very expensive from an HR perspective for a business to try to find qualified and competent technology people—that is, if you can find them, if you know what to do with them, and if you know what to look for in the first place.

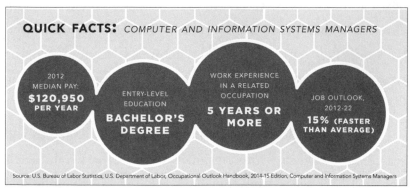

In 2014, The U.S. Bureau of Labor and Statistics reported that the median pay for Information System Managers was well over $100,000. And they are hard to find; job growth for these folks will grow at a pace of 15 percent between 2012 and 2022, outpacing the national average.

Next, how do you even find that technical person even if you do know what to look for? Qualified IT professionals are among the most sought after people by employers anywhere. Finding them and getting them to want to work for you is a challenge.

Don't take it personally, but to a successful IT person, your businesses is probably, well, boring. An in-house IT profession-al's primary job is to keep things working well, and to fix things when they do not. After that happens, and your technology is running smoothly and there are no apparent issues, where is the next challenge?

A business owner will typically purchase new tools and tech-nology only when necessary and generally only when a technology is proven. Often that means leading-edge gadgets are out, and that's no fun for an IT person. Good IT people typically want to be challenged with the latest technology. When things break, they get to practice fixing them. An in-house IT professional will get bored and over time will generally want to look for the next best puzzle or technology. What will you do when the person you hired ultimately gets bored with dealing with your "stale" technol-ogy and decides to move on? You are back to step one. You can also think about it this way: if you have an internal IT person who has successfully stabilized your IT systems, at least for some of the time you will actually be paying them to sit around idly waiting for something bad to happen.

The flip side is that invariably a really strong IT person will search out a company whose primary focus is, that's right, tech-nology. Either a very large company with a seemingly unlimited IT budget, an IT manufacturer, or perhaps a managed services provider, where you, the business owner, should have turned in the first place. I'll explain later just what managed services providers do.

Let's say, however, that you were ultimately successful in hiring and maintaining your own in-house IT staff and you can keep them engaged. Were you able to get adequate coverage? What about nights, weekends, and holidays? Your IT never sleeps but your staff will have to, and sometimes they may even call in sick or want a vacation.

Lastly, what happens when your team gets into trouble with a technology or issue that is beyond their experience? Where do they turn for help? Where can they go?

These are some of the reasons that most small businesses will not be able to attract, afford, and keep really good IT people. That is really the nail in the coffin for the fool's errand of building, staffing, and managing an internal IT department at a small business.

In the final analysis, most people who run or manage a business will be much better off concentrating on running and growing their business, not trying to run their IT networks. And no, I wouldn't act as my own attorney, prepare my business's tax returns, or pull my own tooth either. That's what professionals are for.

THE OUTSOURCING ALTERNATIVES

If you are still reading this book and have gotten this far, you are obviously considering IT outsourcing for your business. The truth is that ultimately, most businesses today, particularly smaller ones between 10 and 250 employees, will decide to enlist some outside support to help navigate these challenging waters. Like many other business support functions, IT outsourcing simply makes sense. When you finally decide to do this with your IT services, you will need to consider several options.

THE INDEPENDENT CONSULTANT

You can hire an individual IT consultant or a team of them. The good news with consultants is that many of them are very experienced with targeted skills (I started out as one myself). They can be great for assistance with a special technology or specific project. However, independent consultants can be hard to find and generally charge a premium—especially if they are good—for their time. And you will be charged for their service most often on an hourly basis. The challenge there is that these independent consultants come with a lot of those same issues as hiring an internal IT department—namely, the need for 24/7 coverage and weekend availability, and too many demands on their time. Often an independent consultant is an expert in one focus area but not others. So an independent consultant is an option but often the weakest one.

MANUFACTURER SUPPORT

What do you do, then, if you have decided that you will neither create your own department nor hire an independent consultant? What is the next option? You can try to acquire IT services and support from each respective IT manufacturer. Dell, Microsoft, HP, IBM, and Cisco all offer high-quality service but generally provide only direct product support for their respective toolsets. They will primarily support their own tools and technologies. In fact, many IT manufacturers depend on an extensive partner network of IT service companies to integrate and support their products. If a technology manufacturer does provide cross-product support, you need to be very careful to avoid the finger-pointing, buck-passing challenge that can arise. By the way, direct manufacturer support, when available, is generally limited and can be very expensive. These folks are not on-site, and their support on hardware or software is typically warranty based. This is another solution but generally not the right one for a small business.

GOING WITH THE BIG GUYS

You can try to acquire outsourced IT strategy and support from one of the big guys. The big guys are very large IT consulting companies or defense contractors such as Lockheed Martin, IBM, Booz Allen Hamilton, SAIC, and others. These companies are all great providers, but they are generally built exclusively to support *other* large companies and large government agencies. You can expect long engagements, expensive and slow, and they generally do not really deal with solutions costing less than seven figures.

They typically will be out of reach for most small business. Why wouldn't a company want to go to these big stalwart companies with legions of IT professionals working for them? The answer is, they don't focus on small businesses and understand them, and they are not capable of supporting them. They will admit it. Serving small businesses is not cost effective for them. They support the government. They support very large companies.

If you are a small business, your challenge is to dive through all these different waters and find the pearl. There may seem to be numerous options for small business IT support, but that is just not the case.

CALLING ON A CARRIER

You can try to acquire IT support and help from what is known as a carrier. A carrier is a big Internet connectivity company, like Verizon, AT&T, Comcast, Time Warner Cable, and Cox. A lot of those folks are trying to get into the small business support and services business.

Similar to a manufacturer, carriers are typically built to support their own connectivity services. If you have a Cox Internet connection, you can call Cox. If you have a Comcast Internet connection, you can call Comcast. But if you are a business with a variety of technologies, who are you going to call about your issue? It is still a problem. And honestly, the carriers have not always been known for their great customer service.

CLOUD PROVIDERS

From email to data backup, the business community is looking more and more to the cloud for solutions. Cloud leaders include Microsoft, Google, Rackspace, and Amazon, and there are an ever increasing number of start-ups.

When it comes to IT strategy and support, however, cloud providers—like IT manufacturers and carriers—tend to provide service centered on their own products and services. If your business can rely on just a single hosted application, then you may be able to depend on that cloud provider for service and support, too. But the irony here is that while most cloud providers are good at providing software, service is usually left to those do-it-yourselfers who like wading through website FAQs and watching YouTube self-help videos. We've discussed the DIY challenges at length in this chapter.

THE MANAGED SERVICES PROVIDER

So where should a business leader turn to find a competent, one-stop shop solution for all its IT needs? The solution that many small businesses are finding is what's known as an IT managed services provider, or simply an MSP.

The concept of managed services is, essentially, outsourcing. In the information technology world, a managed services provider is a company that provides comprehensive IT support, either partially or completely. A key aspect of providing a managed service to a business is that the provider, and not the business, is ultimately responsible for the smooth operation of the service that is outsourced.

THE BEGINNINGS OF THE MSP

We weren't always called "managed services providers." Years ago many of us started as, you guessed it, IT consultants. Some of us banded together to form companies that specialized in providing IT support to small businesses. (In Chapter 4 we'll discuss some of the methods we used to support them.) As the industry has matured over the last 20 years, so have we. System integrators, value added resellers (VARs), and help desk providers are just some of the labels given to us during this time.

What is a managed service?

A managed service is a strategy of outsourcing the day-to-day responsibilities of a critical business function usually with the goal of improving operations and cutting expenses.

What is a managed service provider?

In the information technology world, a managed service provider is a company that provides partially or fully outsourced IT support and management as a fully comprehensive service.

As technology got more complex and indispensable, MSPs were born (or morphed) to provide a consistently delivered IT service to customers who needed a single place to go for all their technology challenges.

Today, a successful MSP has the following four features:

1. "One-stop shop" for all technical customer needs

2. Simple to understand billing options, pay only for what you use, often at a fixed or targeted price

3. Reliance on technology as much as people to service customers

4. Emphasis on providing forward-looking strategy as well as high-quality support

If an MSP is doing its job right, it will be seen as an integral part of the business. The MSP should be thought of as the trusted advisor on all information technology issues.

But, like many things in life, not all management service providers are created equal. You need to make sure that your IT provider can talk cloud and mobility and security and about all of the issues that matter to you. And you need to pay just as much attention, or more, to the kinds of services and support you are getting.

In this chapter, you have seen the rationale in favor of IT out-sourcing and my strong advice not to pull your own teeth when you have a toothache. Now, the question is this: What do you get when you do outsource? What options are we going to be considering?

CHAPTER 4

IF **IT** AIN'T BROKE: TRADITIONAL TECH SUPPORT

Since the time that man began making things, those things have been breaking down. Prehistoric inventors faced broken spears and arrows with frustration, as did ancient explorers who spread their technology around the world. Breakdowns became ever more evident during the Industrial Revolution, with its locomotives and steam engines and printing presses. Whole industries were born whose only purpose was to support the machines, engines, and devices of their age.

When it comes to technology there is one universal truth: every machine eventually will break down, and the more complex the technology, the more likely it is to fail. In the age of information technology, this reality can be costly.

The personal computer, the ubiquitous machine of small business technology, was introduced by IBM on August 12, 1981—and small business IT support started August 13, the very next day.

So who would do the fixing? At first, people assumed that an IBM technician would come with each new IBM personal computer. After all, IBM had previously been the lead manufacturer of mainframe computers to large corporations and government institutions. And mainframes certainly didn't run themselves; they typically came with a small army of support technicians. It must have been quite a shock to many businesses who invested in new "personal computer" systems only to discover that technical support for the new machines was, basically, nonexistent.

It may then have seemed logical that the responsibility for installing and troubleshooting these new devices should fall to the person who had been servicing the office copier or the fax machine. Maybe that person had some experience with radios and electronics and understood what a floppy drive was. That person soon became the in-house "expert."

Such was the early form of tech support at the dawn of the business computing era. The unglamorous job fell to the person who seemed most able to handle it, in what often amounted to an unlucky lottery. If you were the one who took that new PC out of the box and endeavored to set it up, you were anointed with the responsibility to keep that baby alive. If you knew how to plug in the printer, you became the PC troubleshooter around the office. If you had half a clue, you felt that tap on your shoulder and heard, "Hey, Bill, how about seeing if you can figure out why this contraption won't fire up…."

In truth, Bill knew little more than Jim or Sally or anyone else around the office about what needed to be done to nurture the technology. Certainly, none of them knew what would be coming in the years ahead.

THE AGE OF SELF-SERVICE

That's how it was for small businesses for a while, with few places to go for support. I've discussed how the very large businesses that had the mainframes and connected systems received technology support straight from the hardware manufacturer as a bundled part of the mainframe solution.

Small businesses didn't get nearly that much. One reason was that there weren't widely available personal computing devices prior to 1981 that were geared for small business. The most popular and widely available computer before the PC was the Apple II, which really was designed as a hobby computer for people to play with in their homes.

The first real business computer was that IBM model. IBM did it kind of as a lark, a means of putting a toe into the small business industry. There wasn't a lot of software that could be run on it, and few applications. But buying the Big Blue felt safe, and folks were looking to a leader.

When the PC was introduced, it was really intended to be a self-service device. It was expected not to be so complex that it would break often. However, if it did need troubleshooting, you really were left, at first, to rely on your own ability to figure it out.

As people soon realized they couldn't figure it all out, a plethora of support avenues started to emerge where previously there had been virtually none for small businesses. Again, it had been the in-house guru, who generally was self-taught, who was called upon to correct problems as they arose. And if the guru was stumped, the office had plenty of backup systems. The reliance on that PC wasn't nearly as great as it has become today. People pulled out their calculators and dictation machines. They sandwiched carbon paper between sheets of stationery and typed away. They kept that pen handy in the shirt pocket. They were still comfortable with the tools of pre-PC era, but that was all about to change.

HERE COME THE CONSULTANTS

The PC was a huge and immediate success. Soon, new application software was flooding the market through the hundreds of companies that had literally sprung up overnight to capitalize on this new magic box. By 1984 IBM had generated $4 billion in annual PC sales, and a cottage industry of thousands of independent consultants and small unaffiliated companies had developed around the new IBM PC. What was really interesting about this was that these people didn't work for IBM! What a change this was from the old days of only Big Blue computers, Big Blue software, and Big Blue technicians. That was the world back when large mainframe computers were first introduced to the world in the 1960s and 1970s. Everything a large corporation purchased regarding a computer system would be from the same source, namely IBM.

But when IBM introduced the PC in 1981, they also released all its documentation to the world—for free. The first independent consultants studied the "open architecture" of the IBM PC and shared that knowledge with others, and soon an ecosystem developed among customers, developers, and support professionals, all to sustain a device that was no longer tethered to its original manufacturer. This kept costs down and opened up the technology to everyone. While commonplace today, this was a huge step in 1981 by IBM and a big risk for Big Blue at the time.

So when a company purchased several PCs they would look to a PC consultant to help them hook it all together. And when issues arose, they would simply call (or page) their favorite PC consultant.

An early Dataprise brochure from 1997 offering a variety of technology services similar to what an independent consultant of the time would offer. Note the pen in the man's pocket—that's not me.

AN INDUSTRY EMERGES

Tech service continued to be reactive for a long while, meaning that when you had a problem, you called a consultant for help. During these early years, PC service and support for small business was generally provided by individuals for individual systems. Think about it this way: the worst thing that could go wrong with your individual system was for it to crash. Sure, you couldn't complete that spreadsheet or document, but your troubles rarely affected anyone else (unless someone else was waiting on that document). There were no computer viruses to infect the network, no websites that couldn't be accessed, and no shared files that couldn't be viewed.

Only later, as we've seen with the explosion of the Internet and Internet-based applications like email, did the PC move from being a sort of back office or administrative device to being the forefront productivity and collaboration machine that it is today. As the PC and PC networking exploded and mushroomed into prominence, so did the need for service and support. Tech support has burgeoned into an absolutely critical small business function.

As inventors and consumers have known since those days in the caves, the more complex a device, the more support it needs. It takes more know-how to make an arrowhead out of bronze than to make it out of flint. Information technology has become the prime example of an ever-increasing complexity that needs ever more support.

In the early days when people were first designing personal computers, they really didn't think about their maintenance. The hardware designers focused on hardware, the software designers focused on software, and the designers of peripherals, such as printers and scanners and mice and monitors, focused on their things. No one group made all these things work together.

The closest that we've seen to date of one manufacturer taking a shot at perfecting all the different avenues of small business computing would probably be Apple, which has developed and designed their own hardware, their own operating software, and their own peripherals. They have a closed ecosystem, a continuous loop of hardware, software, and peripherals that they control. That's one of the reasons that Apple has risen to prominence as one of the lowest maintenance family of devices ever to hit the market.

The flip side is that because of that same proprietary loop of hardware, software, and peripherals, the rest of the industry—the third party developers and application folks—have not flocked to Apple. On the one hand, Apple has had fewer complaints, fewer viruses, fewer security breaches, and less general failure than the venerable PC and the PC-related technologies. But at the same time, the PC market has more native applications and more software and systems, by an order of magnitude of perhaps a thousand to one. In recent years, however, Apple has worked hard to make up this deficit with its ingenious App Store concept.

So if you control A to Z on a system, you are less likely to have failure and problems and support needs. On the other hand, if you have a more open architecture, like the PC, you will have more adoption and access and more support by the application community.

When the PC arrived, with it came tens of thousands of developers writing their own business software packages, which never seemed to work correctly. The age of tech support was upon us.

REACTIVE VS. PROACTIVE SUPPORT

Business-grade IT support can be characterized primarily in two ways, proactive or reactive. The reactive model—waiting for something to break before it gets fixed—is intuitive and the mainstay in a lot of traditional support environments and is symbolized most commonly by the familiar action of calling the help desk when something goes wrong with your computer.

This use-as-needed approach has been around since the beginning of the technology era. While seemingly the most affordable option (you only pay when using the tech support folks, for example), being reactive can actually be much more costly in the end. That's because when an issue does occur, it can be very expensive to fix, not to mention the cost of lost productivity and downtime.

In contrast, proactive support offers a business the ability to head off problems before they occur. However, this usually means paying more money up front, even when things are going smoothly, in order to keep them that way.

Think about the two differing models this way. When your house roof leaks, you call a roofer to climb up there to find out what's going on. This is reactive. You might do some preventive, or proactive maintenance, but most homeowners aren't thinking that way about the roof.

Conversely, with your car, if you're smart, you bring it in every 3,000 to 6,000 miles and get the oil and filter changed and the scheduled service. That's proactive maintenance—you're trying to head off issues with your car before they happen.

Of course, there are some kinds of problems in your house that you can try to handle proactively, such as termite control. And there will be issues with your car that you won't be able to deal with proactively, as when a nail flattens a tire. There are lots of examples of proactive and reactive support in the traditional world. One of the main differences between the two is cost. Proactive support is often more expensive; it is generally cheaper to have somebody come in, reactively, when something is broken.

This is doubly true with the beginnings of small business computing with PCs, because the technology that surrounded it was more straightforward. You basically had a PC, a connection to the Internet over a modem, and a connection to a printer. Later, perhaps you were networked and had your files attached to a server. That basic configuration and lesser complexity all lends itself to reactive support.

THE BREAK/FIX MODEL OF IT SUPPORT

Another way to look at reactive support in the IT world is what we providers call "break/fix." Break/fix very simply means that when a system, network, or device has a problem and the user contacts a consultant or network administrator, that person will dispatch a qualified technician to fix it. That's what we call break/fix. You wait until something breaks and then you fix it.

Generally, because it is reactive, the break/fix model costs a business as it is used or needed, and usually break/fix providers charge at an hourly rate or on a retainer basis. It's a pay-as-you-go kind of a model. It's very intuitive. It makes sense.

It's hard to budget, though, because you don't know how much you're going to use at any given time. You may go a month as a small business and use very little break/fix support, or, if you have a bad month and a lot of systems require maintenance or have issues, you may use it a lot. So it's hard to charge or budget your expenses, particularly in the beginning.

That can be a problem for small businesses. It's also very labor intensive, because you're using a human being, a certified experienced technician, to solve problems as they arise. That, too, can be very costly.

Going back 20 years at Dataprise, for example, we initially were oriented toward providing our own technology support services to customers under the break/fix model. That was our primary model, largely because of the tools and the technologies and the abilities of our folks to fix systems. In an attempt to assist our clients in budgeting, we would do our best to prescribe the right amount of support hours needed by the business on a monthly basis. We would use our knowledge of a customer's environment and our previous experience with them, if any, to provide a reasonable monthly budget estimate of work that would be required. But in the end, it was really just an educated guess.

THE OLD CASH COW

There's no better example of reactive IT break/fix, especially in the last 10 or 15 years, than what I call the Exchange cash cow. The Exchange cash cow refers to Microsoft's wildly popular email server system used by millions of business users worldwide.

Before Exchange was made available remotely via a cloud hosting provider such as Microsoft's Office 365 platform, it was sold generally as software that would be installed locally on a customer's own server. To a non-expert, Exchange can be a nightmare to initially configure and administer, but it's extremely functional and is used almost universally by businesses large and small. The traditional way to get Microsoft Exchange installed would be to hire a computer consultant, who after spending a significant amount of time installing the Exchange server system, would also install and configure the Exchange Outlook client program on each user's PC. A typical billing arrangement might be to charge an hourly rate or a project fee for the installation.

Exchange and Outlook are great tools. They do a lot more than just send and receive email. The integrated system manages your contacts, your tasks, and your calendar schedules, to name just a few of the things it does. Invariably, the computer consultant would finish the installation, test access to the email for each user, perhaps give a little bit of training, and then leave.

The next day the users would come into the office and have questions about how to open up different attachments or share their calendars, how to import a list of their contacts, and how to create their email signatures. In more recent years, they might need help in trying to sync their mobile phone or mobile device.

What they would be told would be, "No problem. Call the help desk or call your computer consultant." They would be told a qualified technician would walk them through the process, maybe even on that same day.

With every interaction and every user question, another hourly bill would be generated. Exchange is one of those tools in the trade that computer consultants and IT providers refer to as "the gift that keeps on giving" because of its universality but also because of its complexity.

It has also been the bane of existence for many a business that has been strapped with large support bills for what should otherwise be a very straightforward tool. And as reliance on corporate email has grown, so too has an organization's dependence on messaging systems such as Exchange and Outlook. The result of all this is that the break/fix model traditionally has been very good for the IT provider and not so good for the small business.

On the day Microsoft announced that Exchange would now be available directly from the cloud through Office 365, I thought: "There are going to be a lot of out-of-work Exchange consultants out there."

ACCOUNTABILITY

Another issue with the break/fix model is that it's hard to hold your IT service provider accountable.

As I said, when something breaks, we fix it, but who's to say that it shouldn't be breaking time and time again? If something gets fixed, you expect it not to break again, but it's hard for a person that's not an experienced IT professional to really understand all the intricacies and all the different combinations of the different tools that he or she uses.

It's a lot easier for an IT person to fix something one day and then fix something that's related the next day. It's hard for the customer to tell whether or not they're being treated fairly by an IT service provider.

Of course, the vast majority of IT providers are very reputable and honest brokers of the services that they provide, but there's nothing to hold us accountable when you're being billed by the hour.

But it's not just about fixing issues as they arise. Today, you need more from your IT provider—much more. To compete and win in the digital economy, you need to be a *technology-enabled* business. Not just for the IT basics like email, document storage, and network printing, but rather, IT needs to be fundamentally woven into the fabric of your business processes.

In the old days, an attorney might send you a case document by mail or fax machine. Today, clients expect digitally scanned files that can be easily downloaded. You expect your bank to show you yesterday's deposits online including copies of actual checks. And your customers are probably starting to clamor to see all their purchases and want the ability to check in with you online anytime.

You need your IT provider to be showing you the way in this new environment. Holding us accountable for not just making sure things work, but also for helping you to know where to lead your business through the technology jungle, is the new reality.

DOES IT EVER PAY TO BE "REACTIVE"?

If you are a very small business or a small business where technology is used only as a supplemental tool, the break/fix or traditional model may not be all that bad for you. Spending money as issues arrive may actually work to your advantage. An example might be a landscaping company whose operations are primarily outdoors with only a small back office.

Another example of a good candidate for reactive tech support might be smaller businesses with a more sophisticated employee or user base that is more comfortable with technology. Let's say that these businesses have up-to-date or newer PCs and related systems. Let's say that they have a lot of faith in their solid IT support provider.

If that's the case, paying as you go to maintain or fix smaller issues as they arise might be an acceptable model if the overall budget that you've allocated for tech support is by and large kept. There are times when paying as you go makes sense, rather than paying for a more proactive approach. This is particularly true if your technology environment is stable, working, and doesn't change all that often.

An analogy to this might be with health insurance where some businesses decide to be self-insured because of the demographics of their employee base rather than paying a lot more money in premium health insurance.

As I've discussed, it's not a question of "if" you're going to need some support with small business technology. The question is, "When and how much and to what extent?" and also "How much will it hurt me if one of my systems fails?" In a business that is completely network dependent, like a retail store, where cash registers are now really just high-end computers, a problem with a point-of-sale cash register system might mean a loss of revenue or inability to process transactions from customers in your store.

That might require a small business to spend more money to have more proactive support that is being called upon more regularly. Conversely, in our example, the landscaping operation with a small back office, where most of its employees are actually out mowing lawns or trimming gardens, would not necessarily see an immediate impact on the operations of the business if they had a problem with one of their systems or computers.

Basically, IT support—especially reactive support—is like purchasing insurance. It comes down to who you are and what your tolerance is for support problems and the speed that they are resolved. Think of it as turning the dials—one dial for dollars that you want to spend on tech support, and another dial for your tolerance for outages. As a small business owner, you turn those dials to find the right coverage for you. Like insurance, the break/fix or traditional support model lends itself to those kinds of questions and considerations.

At Dataprise, I have some clients where the business owner has decided that it is acceptable to be down for, say, up to 24 hours even if there's a big problem. Therefore, they pay less and are comfortable with a lower level of service. Then I have other clients, such as a doctor's office or a law firm, where they need to be up and running and redundant, without any downtime. They're willing to pay not just for reactive support but for proactive support and maintenance as well.

You need to assess your own business risk tolerance. That is something that your IT provider should help you with in discussing options available to you as a small business.

You have to be willing and able to ask those questions and get those answers up front. If you don't ask, you might be prescribed a type of support that ultimately does not fit your risk tolerance profile or your budget. You need to think through your needs and your tolerance in advance and your potential expenses if things go wrong.

ALONG COMES THE CLOUD

The recent advent of cloud computing has disrupted the traditional break/fix support model and potentially sounded the death knell of those types of reactive services. It has forced both providers and businesses' customers alike to look for a better solution.

Here's why. Those businesses that have started to adopt cloud computing find two things. First, moving some of their local technology resources to a remote-based cloud system can be liberating and cost effective. Second, their reliance on those cloud-based resources skyrockets.

Consider again the Exchange cash cow, where you have Outlook installed locally on your PC and an Exchange email server in your office.

Now, Microsoft's Office 365 has Exchange and Outlook available via the Internet in a cloud-based format. Several immediate technology changes come to mind. First, you don't have to pay to have a computer consultant install an email server. Second, you don't have to pay for the email server. You are renting access to Microsoft's email cloud, called Office 365, and you pay as you use it.

The whole expense of a capital investment disappears. You only pay for what you use. If you have 50 users in your office and they need 50 mailboxes, you pay for 50 mailboxes. If you grow by 15 users, then you add 15 mailboxes.

It's very similar to how you pay a utility, like the electric or gas company. You only pay for what you use. That has been the first big benefit of cloud computing. You don't have to have a capital investment.

The second benefit is that tech support is largely included, as in the Microsoft example. Providers like Microsoft bundle a significant portion of the tech support right into the service, particularly for basic maintenance. You don't have to pay for the software. You don't have to pay for the servers and databases. You don't have to pay for technical problems related to the application itself. The only thing you have to pay for are the users and devices that you use, like your office PC, to connect to your email.

Caution: Use of the cloud does not mean no technology support is required. It just means that the basic support needed has been significantly lessened. You still need end-user training and support, administration of different applications, security, and integration with other systems. Most importantly, you need to ensure that all the technical "plumbing"—meaning the connection between your devices and the cloud-based service such as Office 365—is running smoothly and around the clock.

Nonetheless, the basic operation and maintenance of a cloud-based product like Office 365 is left to the provider and is included with their cloud service fee. Right off the top, your expenses and the total costs of ownership are going to go down.

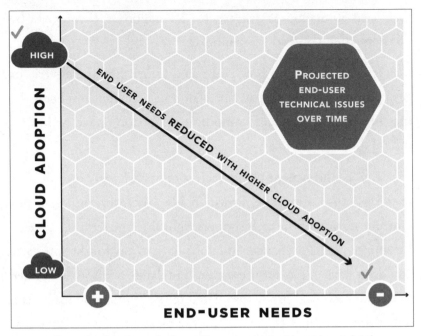

The promise of cloud computing from an IT support perspective is less end-user technical issues over time. We will need to all wait and see if this ultimately is the case.

Cloud computing has shifted the entire landscape of traditional tech support and forced all providers, including my own company, to start thinking about being more proactive and realigning the way that we deliver that support.

IT SUPERHEROES

If we don't get invited to your Christmas or holiday party, we say at Dataprise, then we must be doing something wrong.

In all fairness, the traditional break/fix model of IT services, which I've discussed in this chapter, is certainly not always all bad. We have many clients still on a traditional IT support model who are very happy with it. They feel a sense of stability as our skilled people and technical resources and become part of the family.

They are comfortable with the assigned technicians whom they have come to know and trust.

In my experience, just because something new is on the horizon is not always a good reason for change. There needs to be some motivating factor, whether it's saving money, efficiency, or an event, such as when you move, expand, or lose or gain employees. The motivation might even be a new way of doing things, such as the move towards cloud computing. Those would be good reasons to consider changing the way you do your IT support.

A big benefit of the traditional model, however, is that we're embedded in the company. Your engineer becomes your superhero. We become part of the culture of your organization, and that consistency and personal touch is a tremendous benefit. That traditional model is available from many managed services providers today, and we're happy to provide it to anyone who still wants it.

To reiterate the disadvantages, however, this model is a very reactive way of doing business. It's better in any business endeavor to be proactive, and that holds true for your IT services. To simply react to situations means you aren't heading off issues and problems. You aren't facing them until you are confronted with them, and that's no way to stay ahead of the competition. You need to anticipate and take decisive action well in advance—and technology is key to maintaining that competitive advantage.

You don't know what's going to break until it breaks. What it will take to fix the problem is also variable—and therefore, under the traditional model, the amount you will pay for those bills is variable as well. Meanwhile, you face the prospect of the dreaded downtime—which a business should want to avoid at any level in technology. A lot of people can relate to what happens if email is not working or mobile phones can't connect or the Internet has gone down.

And because this model is labor dependent, if that embedded technician leaves—gets reassigned, graduates, or quits—then you've potentially lost your connection to that traditional support mechanism. A good managed services provider will have a bench of talent from which to supply you someone new, so that the impact of losing your primary technician or consultant is minimal. Still, you are losing someone you came to trust—and now it's somebody new that you'll be inviting to the party.

NOT ALL TECHIES CREATED EQUAL

Those tech guys and gals are not all created equal when it comes to experience in IT. Will your technician have the depth of experience to really help you leverage your technology investments to the maximum? If you don't know what you're buying, you well might end up buying too much, a pervasive problem in the industry. It's like buying an expensive race car when you need a jeep. Both will get you where you want to go, but you may only need the jeep.

The expertise that a trained technologist can bring to bear is not just making sure that you minimize your downtime. You also get an advantage over your competition, depending on the person's experience and judgment. But you can't really know who you are getting by looking at credentials. It's hard for the general IT consumer to differentiate who's good and who's not.

In the health care industry or the legal profession or the financial accounting industry, people are licensed or certified and have the governmental or regulatory credentials that the industry and customers, in general, can rely upon. But there really is no similar credential system across the board for IT professionals.

Major manufacturers like Cisco and Microsoft and Dell and a lot of others offer their own specific vendor certifications. However, many other technology providers do not. And even if a technician is, for example, Microsoft certified, that does not necessarily mean that they are versed in other manufacturers' technologies.

So it's very compartmentalized. You don't know if the technician has the experience and depth to handle your problems day in and day out and year to year. There is no centralized accreditation or licensing authority.

That's not to say that there are not a lot of sophisticated training and programs out there. Leading institutions offer four-year degrees in management of information systems, or computer science or information technology. Consumers and employers and business owners could feel assured of people with a solid academic background—but a lot of people in our industry don't go the university route. A lot are self-taught or get vocational training. They're in such demand that they can get a high-paying job in IT without the traditional four-year schooling.

While the cost of a resource can sometimes indirectly indicate a technician's experience, when working with a support provider that has blended rates, you won't always know whom you are going to get. You still can't really discern if the person you are getting has the desired experience.

THE FUTURE OF IT SUPPORT

A lot of people think that when they move to the cloud, they can fire the tech support guy. Not so fast: You're still going to have support issues, security issues, training issues, administration issues, and data issues—a variety of concerns to resolve on a continuing basis. No matter where your "stuff" resides—in the cloud or in your office—it is still going to require some level of technology support.

In this new era, one solution is to provide IT support as a fully outsourced managed service. The future in support will be to proactively monitor the technology wherever it is found, and billing will be based on the number of things being managed, not the number of hours provided—and that will be far easier for small businesses to budget.

The future in support will be an accountable system of service where the risk does not fall entirely on the customer. It will fall on the provider as well, who must spend as many hours as it takes to keep the system running, all for a predictable monthly fee—a much better partnership between customer and provider.

In the pages ahead, we'll be taking a closer look at that future. We'll look at the details of IT service and support as a fully managed service.

CHAPTER 5

IT MANAGED SERVICES: A NEW AND IMPROVED RECIPE

With the maturation of business technology and the growth of cloud computing, IT service and support have seen significant change as well—and I would say for the better.

Since around 2007, a different model has been evolving, called IT managed services. An IT managed services agreement involves paying not on a variable hourly basis, as is generally found in the break/fix model, but more often paying on a per-device or per-user basis with all of the relevant IT support and services included.

That's a very important point: Whereas with the traditional model, hourly support is basically charged by the quantity of service provided (for example, billed by the number of service hours worked), the managed services model is generally built on the number of systems or users that the IT service provider is managing. Recall that this is the same concept I discussed earlier related to how cloud providers—like utility companies—charge their customers only for what is used. IT managed services is based on that same concept.

In the traditional model, the number of hours spent is prescribed by the provider depending on what they think is the best fit for the customer—maybe 24 or 32 hours or more per month of support. It's used as needed. By contrast, in the new IT managed services model, you just count the number of devices or users to determine how much is billed.

In addition, most managed services agreements are all-inclusive of services related to the users or devices. That results in price predictability. You only get charged based on the quantity of devices or users under management, and all the services needed for that device or user are included.

In the business world, the needle has moved from a break/fix model to a fully managed and inclusive model, also called the unlimited support model, one of the major benefits of the managed services approach. That's a big transition.

Under traditional break/fix, a business might suspect that there isn't really an incentive to keep things working all that well because the provider is paid more when things break. But with managed services, the provider is paid the same whether things are broken or working smoothly.

At Dataprise, we try to put the right fit to the right customer. But at the end of the day, under the break/fix model, if something breaks the second and third and fourth time, it is going to get fixed for a second and third and fourth time, and you're going to get a second and third and fourth bill. Under the new model, we're going to charge you X amount per device, all-inclusive. The clock is off.

Service Automation—A Recipe for IT Managed Services

We've come a long way from the days of depending only on a technician and his toolbox. Here is a typical recipe for how a fully managed service is provided: Many new small businesses are now "born in the cloud." Here are some suggestions of popular freeware or "cheapware" Internet sites to get you started:

1. Remote Monitoring & Management software agents are installed on every managed device (such as desktops and servers).

2. "Alerts" are configured for each type of device. When an issue is detected the agent automatically sends the alert to the MSP monitoring center or help desk.

3. The help desk takes action proactively when an alert is received. In many cases users are unaffected and don't even realize a potential problem has been averted.

4. When a manufacturer issues a software patch or advises the MSP of a security risk, the MSP help desk proactively installs patches, often at night, to ensure systems keep running smoothly.

5. When a user does have an issue or problem that has not been automatically detected, he or she can contact the help desk 24/7. A qualified technician will open a ticket and work remotely using screen-sharing software to resolve the issue in real time with the user.

6. If a problem persists or cannot be resolved remotely, the MSP will dispatch a technician on-site to resolve the problem. ⬡

It has now become much easier for a small business to antici-pate what they're going to pay. There's no more cash cow. The provider gets the same pay whether they spend 100 hours support-ing a PC or 1 hour. They figure: "We're going to do the best job we can to ensure that the system is running up to speed, because if it's not, we're going to spend more of our resources in making sure that it is, and at no additional cost to you."

CATALYST FOR CHANGE

Why is this happening now? If it weren't for the cloud, we would probably still be talking about break/fix support. That has been the reason that the managed model has come to fruition. It may have come anyway without the cloud, but the cloud has hastened it in.

Today, what you see in the IT service provider industry coast to coast and even worldwide is a flurry of providers moving their clients from the traditional break/fix support model to a more managed model.

The managed model can be very beneficial to the provider as well, because the provider profits by getting better at handling different types of issues. Once the provider learns how to fix something the first time, they can apply those fixes across an entire customer base. Like most things, a job well done should be profitable.

The managed services model is one of those rare win-wins, though it does have its challenges. It's not perfect, as I will explain. But we clearly have moved from an expensive and labor-intensive model to an "all you can eat" model. That transition really started to take off across the industry in recent years, fueled by the cloud and related technologies.

Managed services is proactive because we're not going to wait until something breaks. With a managed services provider, we are connected to a customer's systems in real time, all the time. We monitor and manage remotely.

We call this RMM, remote monitoring and management, of a client's computer systems. A suite of software monitoring applications allow us to do that. We're going to see alerts and issues and problems as they arise on your computer, usually back at our help desk or network operations center (NOC). It is essential for the provider to be proactive in order to make money on a managed services customer. If we wait until a problem arises—a disk runs out of space, a virus infects your files, you suffer a security breach, or some other issue—we're going to spend a lot more time and effort fixing that issue than we would if we had been alerted automatically through RMM software.

It's similar to managed health care. It ultimately costs a lot more unless doctors deal with patients proactively with checkups and vaccinations and prophylactic methods before those patients get sick with a critical and risky problem that consumes a lot more time, effort, and money. In the managed care model, the provider is proactive in order to be cost effective. It has been a revolutionary change in modern health care. The incentive now is switching toward making the patient healthier so that you don't have to spend as much money on that patient. When you're getting a fixed price, preventive care somehow rises in importance.

It's not just the cloud that has enabled the managed services support model. Along with the advent of cloud computing, technology in general has gotten better. In his 1995 book The Road Ahead, Microsoft founder Bill Gates said technology would ultimately cost less to own and maintain. He presented his views of the decreasing total cost of technology ownership over time—he called it TCO. Almost two decades later, much of what Gates forecast has proven true.

Managed services providers can do their job because of advances in remote monitoring and rapid problem resolution.

They generally use the Internet and monitoring software to operate the remote help desk. They can connect to your PC via the Internet to solve problems and to push software patches and update virus checks, all by remote control. They can initiate a two-way screen-sharing session to help provide you with answers directly on your desktop.

Today a remotely located support technician can render assistance by directly connecting to an affected user's desktop over a secure Internet connection. Through modern screen-sharing technology, the tech will see exactly what the user sees on screen and will thus be able to more rapidly resolve an issue.

With improved technology, gone are the days of constant PC reboots and lockups, including the dreaded Microsoft Windows "blue screen of death." These things still happen but much less frequently. PCs can sometimes self-heal by automatically updating themselves at night with the manufacturer's latest fixes and software patches right over the Internet. And when problems do arise, the sophisticated RMM software allows a technician to remotely monitor and fix small issues before they become major ones. This is the future of proactive IT support.

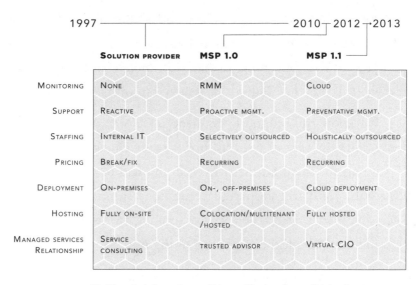

	1997 ————————————— 2010 ┬ 2012 ┬ 2013		
	SOLUTION PROVIDER	**MSP 1.0**	**MSP 1.1**
MONITORING	NONE	RMM	CLOUD
SUPPORT	REACTIVE	PROACTIVE MGMT.	PREVENTATIVE MGMT.
STAFFING	INTERNAL IT	SELECTIVELY OUTSOURCED	HOLISTICALLY OUTSOURCED
PRICING	BREAK/FIX	RECURRING	RECURRING
DEPLOYMENT	ON-PREMISES	ON-, OFF-PREMISES	CLOUD DEPLOYMENT
HOSTING	FULLY ON-SITE	COLOCATION/MULTITENANT /HOSTED	FULLY HOSTED
MANAGED SERVICES RELATIONSHIP	SERVICE CONSULTING	TRUSTED ADVISOR	VIRTUAL CIO

The Three Evolutionary Stages of Managed Services. Source: "Market Overview: Managed Service Providers, Part 2", Forrester Research, Inc., May 6, 2013

DEMANDS OF A TOUGH ECONOMY

To briefly recap why this switch has occurred: The economic crash of 2009 heralded in the modern era for managed services providers. In the United States, businesses of all types were laying off employees and struggling. Business owners couldn't afford to make new capital investments in technology and training, so it was essential to keep running what they had. Those that couldn't staff their own IT department sought outside advice and assistance, usually from a managed services provider.

Then, cloud computing came on the scene and offered needed relief to struggling businesses through its utilities-based, or "pay as you go for only what you need" model. This new era of "rent, not buy," particularly business software applications, was here to stay. In the recession, people were more willing to try new ways of running their IT. If you had only $20,000 and could spend that

$20,000 to buy two new servers or spend $1,000 a month to rent software over the Internet from a cloud provider, what were you going to do? You were going to save your money and rent instead of own. This was the catalyst that ushered in the "cloud era."

We know the economic crash of 2009 was devastating for the country, in a lot of respects, but it really changed the face of IT support for small business. Even if you had to let go some of your staff, you'd still keep your technology running. The Great Recession inaugurated a new way of looking at business technology, and that's about the only silver lining to it.

Along with the cloud era and its notion of pay only for what you use, came the idea of utility-based managed support, a new way of doing things. It matched the demand of a tight economy and tight budgets and short staffs, and it also matched the demands of a rapidly changing technology. Who wants to own when what you buy could soon be outdated?

SHARED RISK

Businesses started realizing that marrying up with an MSP is a great strategy for all those reasons. It makes the most sense for businesses that lack the resources for creating their own in-house IT department.

One of the biggest benefits of this new type of partnership is the concept of shared risk. The risk and the cost of supporting technologies has moved significantly off of the customer, which is what you typically see in the traditional model, and at least partially onto the MSP—and that's great for the customer. If you call us repeatedly to come out and do repairs, we lose, because you pay only the set fee based on number of employees or devices. Unless you ask for additional services, that's all that you will have to pay.

That is how the risk has moved from the customer to the provider.

PROACTIVE ISN'T PERFECT

Like anything, there are drawbacks. One significant drawback of the managed, fully inclusive model is that MSPs are not incentivized to be as embedded with their customers, as in the traditional model. MSPs do not make money when they're busy on-site or on the phone "helping" their customers. They make money when the systems that they have put in place run smoothly on their own and have no issues. That's because they get paid the same whether they have to spend a lot of time with you or little time.

THE IT SUPPORT PARADOX

The greatest benefit of traditional break/fix support is that a provider is economically incentivized to "reach out and touch" his customer often, with the highest skilled and attentive individuals as possible. Conversely, in a fully managed fixed price or per-seat managed support model, the IT provider is financially motivated to provide his customer with minimally acceptable service. This includes fewer and less technical people, fewer client interactions and touches, and sometimes a seemingly overreliance on technology-based systems, such as monitoring and remote management.

In other words, under this new unlimited service model the provider manages the customer's IT by being more proactive with RMM automation and a remote help desk. But the provider is no longer motivated to talk to or engage the customer under this arrangement, because the provider gets only a fixed fee per month for all services, regardless of the effort spent. It becomes expensive if a highly paid technician spends too much time having to "touch" the customer. When there is a problem, the process is often to assign the least experienced person first, and if he or she can't fix it, someone with greater skills will be assigned. And this is generally all done remotely from the provider's help desk. Often under a fully managed services plan, a provider won't actually send someone on-site unless they have exhausted all means of remote troubleshooting and diagnosis first. This is how provider costs are minimized and is usually a key aspect of the fully managed model.

That "hands off" management approach can be frustrating for a client who is used to having someone on-site and readily available to assist. As managed services have grown in popularity, this has increasingly become an issue, particularly for smaller businesses. The larger ones might be more used to a utility-based service, or might have adopted a little sooner. But other businesses need more assistance, depending on the industry, and those folks in some cases have complained that they feel left in the dust.

They have been accustomed to seeing Steve or Rachel or Bob frequently in the office, whistling a tune and asking how things are going with their systems and their PCs and their laptops. Now those people aren't regularly at the office. They're in a remote support or help desk center, sometimes far away, monitoring things from afar. That change in culture has big implications on how people perceive the way they are being served. The computer guy does not know your name anymore. He's just some voice on the phone somewhere.

And so despite the built-in incentive to keep the technology running smoothly, the new model of managed service often feels impersonal. What's lost is the human touch. Never mind, for a moment, that the technology has advanced and the monitoring capability is tremendous. Never mind that the proactive approach lets technicians see an automated alert message and fix an issue remotely before you know it even exists. People are still people. They like to interact. This type of stand-off support does not offer that. The fully inclusive managed services can be maddening to those people who require a little bit more interaction.

There's an analogy in the medical field, with advent of managed care. Some doctors offer concierge services. In some modern practices, you check in remotely, via video screen, and you may not even speak to the doctor anymore but rather to a physician's assistant or a nurse. Technology has enhanced the resources and the ability to reach out to more people with efficiency. But people miss the personal touch, and it can feel absent with technology-enabled managed care. Some people can adapt to that. I think the younger generations can more readily accept that way of doing things, but it's harder for people who are used to a certain level of professional services.

Another potential issue in a fully managed support arrangement is that of coverage. In the newer per-seat or per-user model, the customer and provider agree specifically ahead of time as to what is and what is not covered under the managed services agreement. Exact identities and quantities of supported devices, users, and office locations are documented, as are the types of systems and applications you have. Commonplace programs such as word processing, email, and cloud applications are obviously all included, but custom database applications, websites, high-end accounting systems, and older off-warranty hardware may not be. This means that if you have a problem with what the provider considers to be an out-of-scope system or tool, you may find the provider unable or unwilling to support you, at least not under a fixed fee arrangement.

The implication here is that a provider may only want to support you under a fixed fee managed services agreement if your IT is stabilized and fairly up to date and only if you have the most common technologies. Anything not documented and agreed to ahead of time will be considered uncovered or out of scope. That can be a big surprise to a customer if they don't understand this ahead of time. Do you remember our insurance plan analogy? If it's not on the plan, it's not covered.

In the world of fully managed IT, that is the gist of the support paradox that became ever more apparent as a result of the recent economic downturn. As managed services and managed services providers burgeoned, businesses were clearly pleased with the predictable nature of the all-inclusive support under the utility model. No longer did they feel nickel and dimed under the break/fix model, though they often still missed the personalized service of someone who knew their business and staff and inner workings of the organization. When employees asked, "So where's my computer guy?" the answer that he was just a phone call or web click away just didn't seem satisfactory.

There had to be a better way to provide holistic IT support that would also include the personalized, local, and in-touch experiences that business users had gotten used to. There had to be a better way to blend the old and the new—and in the next chapter, we'll take a look at the development of a better hybrid support model.

CHAPTER 6

THE BEST OF ALL WORLDS: THE UNIFIED SERVICE EQUATION

What I've learned in almost 20 years of experience is that we're not all ready for one way of doing things, especially when it comes to IT. We're not all ready to have all of our problems solved remotely through screen-sharing sessions or over the telephone or through a mobile device or through an automatic self-help portal on the web. Many people, young and old, still like the press-the-flesh aspect of having a question asked and a question answered.

The traditional break/fix support scenario had the benefit of personalized service from highly trained IT professionals. The fully managed service approach has the benefit of automation and predictable pricing. If you choose one, you don't get the other. Business owners began asking, "So how do I choose? How can I get what I need for my money?" They wanted to be able to count on having that friendly technician available, but they also wanted to be able to count on a price that they could budget with some assurance.

In other words, they want the human touch, and they also want all of the advantages of a fully managed solution. And, in essence, this is where the industry is heading. I'm proud to say that my company is among the trendsetters that is offering this hybrid approach.

EACH MODEL HAS ITS PLACE

The break/fix or "traditional" model, and the newer fully managed service or "unlimited" model both have a place in IT services. We will provide you whichever service type you like, but if you ask us which one we would recommend, we will say to choose your support options from what we call the unified service equation or USE. We've created the USE formula to stand for a four-part plan that combines the elements of both the old and new schools of thought on providing comprehensive IT support services to business.

We call the USE approach the "Goldilocks" solution because it's neither too hot nor too cold—it's just right for many small businesses. Break/fix and fully managed services both have their advantages and disadvantages, just like most other business practices, but the balanced USE formula combines the best of both worlds.

In previous chapters I've detailed the history of IT support and its Wild West–style origins. I've traced the development of the traditional consulting model for small and medium-sized busi-nesses, the reactive "break/fix" model. As hardware and software evolved and the cloud moved in, we moved to a proactive model of managed support, with bells and whistles such as remote management and monitoring. In a tight economy, customers began demanding fixed pricing, a shared risk approach and more stability on what they were going to spend. We have seen how that has changed the incentives of the industry so that it is in a provider's best interest to keep the technology running flawlessly to prevent the need for providing expensive support resources.

And we have also seen how some customers very much miss that up-close and personal service. The providers, who get the same fee regardless of the amount of service provided, are "touching" their clients less, providing support remotely whenever possible. The paradox is that the new model promotes better technology but less consultative service. The customers can wind up feeling empty in terms of what they were used to.

One way or another, there are advantages and disadvantages but neither model completely satisfies the customer. The old traditional model and the new managed business model each have their drawbacks that leave the customer feeling that something's missing.

In the last five years or so, a lot of customers have nonetheless wanted to move to that model, and a lot of providers have gone to it because, quite frankly, it's easy to sell. Customers are flocking to it. Smaller providers find it particularly easy to engage on a fixed platform. It's somewhat like the health care HMO model that provides service to patients at a lower cost to them with lower deductibles—so long as they stay within the network.

A BALANCED APPROACH

Many in our industry are now moving toward the centerline, coming up with a hybrid service model. At Dataprise our hybrid model is based on our own USE concept. We call it Support365.

Successful providers around the country, small and large, have likewise tried to centerline their approaches in this manner. And if they haven't yet, they probably will. There are different brands and different dials and methods that they use, but they recognize that a polarized approach—either break/fix or the managed model—is not ultimately going to be successful.

| Strategic Consulting | IT Management | Service Desk | Cloud365® Services |

My company promoted the older traditional approach for many years. Because we have been around for almost 20 years, we obviously started off in the traditional model because that's all there was when I started my business. So we were deeply rooted in an on-site embedded approach, with personalized human service. The pendulum has swung away from that approach in the last five to six years, for the reasons I've pointed out.

With some of our clients we tried a strictly remote managed model—but almost every customer ultimately had complaints about that approach. Again, they appreciated the pricing and some of the advantages of a fully managed service, but the top complaint consistently was the lack of personalization.

In response, rather than try to force a new model just because that's the trend, we studied the problem and asked our customers—we have about a thousand of them—for advice. In analyzing the issues, we have found an equalized approach. It borrows the best aspects from the old and the new—and, as with most things in life, that is the best policy.

Many other providers have their own brand of a balanced approach that has moved to the centerline. I believe that as with most things, it's best not to be polarized.

Our managed services solution is based on our unified service equation, which is rooted in our experience and recommended industry best practices. We've incorporated some of the most widely used and adopted IT management structures in use today, including popular service frameworks such as ITIL®. Designed for small businesses specifically, our Support365 USE framework has four primary areas of concentration.

STRATEGIC CONSULTING

IT strategy from a trusted advisor. This is where your business would benefit from the personalized advice of a virtual chief information officer or vCIO. A vCIO would not be someone crawling under desks and inspecting cables; he or she would be tasked with understanding your organization's global technology needs. Then, your vCIO would work with you to provide your business an IT roadmap or plan that would be followed and reported on year after year.

The vCIO would communicate directly with senior management and ensure that new technologies are evaluated, budgets are adhered to, and projects are completed properly.

IT MANAGEMENT

IT infrastructure management is where the rubber hits the road in a proactive managed service. RMM technologies ensure that your business's tech assets are kept running smoothly and if problems do arise, intelligent software agents are used to automatically fix problems as they are detected.

In addition to service automation for routine tasks, IT management also includes the notion of scheduled or routine on-site support when necessary to provide a personalized face to technical support as well as "desk side" assistance to those employees who need some additional help.

SERVICE DESK

When an end user does have a problem, they can contact a 24/7 global help desk for user issue handling and response. The service desk can be contacted by email, chat, and phone. A service desk technician will open a service ticket and use a variety of diagnostic tools to efficiently resolve a user's problem. As we've seen, a key feature of a modern help desk is the use of live screen-sharing software that allows a technician to troubleshoot issues directly with an end user in real time.

CLOUD TOOLS

Using the right management tools can significantly increase the efficiency of any IT support function. Today, cloud-based support tools include:

- Cloud-based backup and disaster recovery solutions
- Remote monitoring and management (RMM)

◆ Incident tracking software

◆ Hosting systems

◆ Self-help portal solutions

Our own Support365 USE framework is forever changing. It's dynamic. There are things that we're always going to revisit. When customers need something new, we look at incorporating a new feature or aspect into our model. When a manufacturer such as Microsoft or Dell comes out with a new software or hardware system that is more self-healing or has new features and technologies that require either more or less support, we incorporate that into the model. We do the same with Internet providers and new cloud technologies.

One recent example of this is VoIP telephony support. VoIP (Voice over Internet Protocol)–based phones are more recent additions to a small business IT arsenal and feature a phone system capable of connecting over an Internet connection. VoIP phones have become fairly commonplace, but the technology is still new enough that many network engineers have not had the adequate training to properly support them. Phones have traditionally been a very specialized office function that were never connected to a data network or LAN in the past. Now, they are. This has forced providers to adapt and to learn how to incorporate VoIP support into their managed service frameworks. This has proven difficult for many IT folks to do.

FLEXIBILITY IS ESSENTIAL

To provide great service under a hybrid model such as the unified service equation, and effective IT support in general, the provider needs to be flexible. A lot of providers are so stuck in one way or the other that they often don't listen to the customer. I think that's one of the valuable takeaways from all this, which is that ultimately it's not the provider's responsibility to force a particular brand of service down the throat of a particular customer. You have to give customers options and allow their needs and their specific issues and requirements to really drive, ultimately, the solution. The conversation must be allowed to flow to the right answers.

For example, a lot of times we start off talking to a customer about their application server needs including support, only to find out that what they're really looking for is a new technology platform that could alleviate the need for that software server in the first place. We often get calls about the possibility of augmenting staff or establishing on-site resources to support old systems, and the discussion ends up being about investing in an upgrade with more suitable and economical means of support.

The ability to listen to the client's needs is important in providing technology support, as it is in most consultative businesses. The solution depends on it. One size does not fit all in technology service. That's an important concept, and yet it's counterintuitive to what a lot of people are saying.

One need only look at the options that are out there for the business consumer, particularly the small to medium-sized business consumer, to see why it is so difficult for a customer to figure out which way to go with technology and support for those technologies.

Cloud providers such as Google and VMware are counting on all things being from the cloud. In their world, the only thing primarily a small business consumer needs is a connection to the Internet and some device to connect to their cloud. You can get all your applications, store all your data, and share all your resources on a cloud platform. In many cases, the support need can be minimal.

For software manufacturers such as Microsoft, the push is software that runs on a PC device, laptop, and server, while also obviously fully embracing the cloud in recent years as well. So their intention or spin is to have consumers focus on their own personal device. Manufacturers like HP and Dell are primarily device developers that try to be independent of where the software runs, whether it's the cloud or locally on the device. They're trying to focus on both.

From a consumer perspective, it becomes more than a matter of one size does not fit all in deciding on the type of technology. It's also that one type of support solution does not fit all. The best solution depends on the type of needs that your business has and the technologies that you embrace. It depends on your budget, the type of users and their sophistication, and your applications and systems.

Numerous variables come into play when trying to figure out your technology investment for your business and how to manage and support it all. And that is why the support cannot be entirely in one direction or the other. One of the first things that people tell me is, "We want to avoid making a big mistake." It is important that their provider be willing to evaluate the consumer's specific needs, as opposed to simply prescribing the only solution it offers.

NOT ALL OR NOTHING

Many business owners I speak with fail to realize that working with an MSP doesn't mean necessarily turning over all the keys to the IT systems. Say your business is at the larger end of the smaller-sized spectrum with a couple of hundred employees, and you have a basic IT support system that works for you. You may have a couple of trusted system administrators on staff that know your current IT needs very well.

But you are growing and as we've discussed, the times they are a-changin, as the old Bob Dylan song goes. You shouldn't have to make a choice necessarily between the old and the new. At least not right away.

FULLY MANAGED IT SUPPORT

We've discussed at length the benefits of connecting with a qualified managed services provider and not building your own IT department. This is the modality that will benefit the vast majority of small businesses from here on out. This book has been primarily about fully outsourced IT services. But there is another style.

CO-MANAGED IT SUPPORT

Co-managed or supplemental support provides a business with choices. You can get your cake and eat it too. This is typically a dual-responsibility arrangement, where the business's internal and existing IT staff handles the traditional needs of the business and the MSP is assigned either frontline or back office responsibilities as the case may be.

Examples of co-managed IT services include:

- ◆ Internal IT staff responsible for on-site support; MSP responsible for remote help desk

- ◆ Internal IT staff responsible for server support; MSP responsible for desktop support

- ◆ Internal IT staff responsible for HQ support; MSP responsible for remote teleworkers and remote office support

And the list goes on. Clear lines of communication and assigned responsibilities are essential components of a successful co-management strategy.

EVOLVING PRICING OPTIONS

One of the biggest drivers in technology service and support, as in most things, is price. And today, pricing options are one of the hottest debated topics among MSPs. Here are several of the more modern pricing options that are evolving almost daily in the IT managed services provider industry.

PER-DEVICE PRICING

In per-device pricing, customers are charged by the number of their total devices under management. "Under management" means those are the devices for which an IT provider is responsible for operation and support.

Under this pricing option, you typically are charged monthly based on how many devices you have. Those charges will vary among PC, desktops, servers, network, and mobile devices. For an example, it is typical to see, say, $25 to $50 per desktop as a monthly charge for unlimited desktop support, and perhaps as much as $300 per server per month.

That fee covers all support related to that device. A typical exception would be hardware parts warranty support, which is usually not included. But everything else is 24/7 and 365 days a year for that device. This generally includes everything up from the "bare metal" of the device, such as operating system, applications, connectivity, security, printing, and so on.

Pricing a fully managed device option is as simple as counting up the number of devices that you want to move to a managed solution and getting a price quotation for that. A big benefit of this type of pricing and the managed model in general is that you only get charged for those devices that you've selected to manage, nothing more.

PER-USER PRICING

The next option is per-user pricing, which many providers are also offering. In per-user pricing, customers are charged by the number of their users, often employees under management. A typical user may be charged up to, say, $50 to $75 per month for unlimited support and access to 24/7 service. Usually the user would be able to bring under management his or her office-related devices, typically more than one.

For an example, if you're in the per-user model, you might have a provider offer you up to, let's say, three devices, such as your PC, your mobile phone, and your laptop. This is sometimes called BYOD or bring-your-own-device support. That's a nice option for companies that know that they've got constituencies or staff that have more than one device. It potentially can save some money.

Rather than having to count up each device, you can count up each employee or user.

SLA PRICING

The next option is SLA or Service Level Agreement based pricing. This option is relatively new and takes a slightly different approach. Basically, a customer pays for the type of service response that they can afford and that they need.

For example, an organization might pay a particular price for business-hour support coverage five days per week, and perhaps a higher fee for 24/7 round-the-clock support. Another example of SLA pricing may involve the queue waiting time of a provider, or how fast the provider guarantees a response to the user's issue.

SLA pricing basically is an option that allows a customer to determine the service levels and the response times. The customer chooses the type of responses they want to get, and the times when those responses will be provided.

VALUE PRICING

Value pricing is the concept of pricing based on the type of services provided. For example, Value 1 pricing might be a help desk service. Value 2 pricing might include help desk service with remote monitoring and management, or RMM. Being able to choose the different pieces of what a business wants is another way to distinguish Service A from Service B.

TERM PRICING

A fifth option is term pricing. Term pricing is the notion of differential pricing based on commitments that the customer is willing to make to an MSP. Typical examples range from month-to-month, one-year, two-year, and even three-year agreements.

Naturally, you would expect that the longer a commitment to a provider, the deeper the discounts and the lower the pricing. Cell phone carriers have similar arrangements. If you want a month-to-month contract, a carrier is going to charge you full price for the phone to recoup expenses. If you're willing to commit to two years, the carrier may toss the phone in for free.

A lot of companies and consumers are wary of being locked into a term agreement. But it can work well and be cost effective if you've got service level agreements and teeth in an agreement where your provider is responsible for providing service in a certain way and having certain satisfaction levels.

Short-term agreements, like month-to-month, do not always give the provider an opportunity to shine, however. It may often take more than a few months to stabilize your particular environment. Generally speaking, providers and customers who are weighted to short-term agreements often, in my view, are not oriented toward a symbiotic or a trusted advisor relationship. It often takes a bit of time to establish the trust that is almost impossible to get in a short-term or month-to-month agreement, particularly if a provider is stepping into an unstable environment. The customers have trouble getting the stability of service and expertise that they desire, and the providers don't get that stable longer term customer that they want.

ENVIRONMENTAL PRICING

Environmental pricing amounts to a monthly price that accounts for everything in your environment, including users, infrastructure, desktops, PCs, mobile devices, servers, locations, and applications—it's the "whole enchilada" pricing.

If a provider is very comfortable with a customer, knows the environment, and perhaps has been supporting that customer for a while in the more traditional model, then this type of pricing is saying, "We know your environment. Here's what we've seen as we have supported you. We will give you a fixed price based on your current situation. Provided your environment does not change—so you're not adding a lot more employees or equipment or infrastructure—then we believe that we can support you holistically for this one price."

In such a case, the provider may take an average of the last two years' monthly payments. The environmental pricing is not the easiest one to calculate, because it requires due diligence on the part of the provider so that they really understand the actual state and quality of the customer's technology. But it is really a tremendous boon for a customer who wants to stay with a provider but wants off the variable pricing model. Environmental pricing may seem a bit obscure, but frankly it's a magic bullet for us and is most often used when we know that your environment is stable and doesn't change that much over time.

Which costs more, new vs. old pricing?

I'm often asked if the newer fully managed IT support model is less expensive than the older and more traditional break-fix model.

The short answer is probably not.

With an unlimited, all-inclusive, 24/7 fixed pricing arrangement, a managed service may often be, on its face, more expensive than hourly service. But remember, this is a shared risk model where before the risk was entirely on you, the customer. Now the provider is also on the line. You are also getting a lot more value for your money in the newer scenario, and over time you should wind up investing less in hardware and software as well. ◆

A MIX OF THOSE PRICING MODELS

Those are the six types of pricing that I've seen in the industry in the last few years in particular. Competent managed services providers are typically providing a mix of these pricing models and options to customers, offering a hybrid that is their own "brand" of managed service.

To distinguish one from another, you don't want to have, in my view, just per-user pricing or just value pricing. The real solution and the real benefit is an intelligently selected mix of the different aspects of pricing and options that mean the most to you as a customer.

You need the guidance and support and advice of a professional to allow you to see the different benefits of these options. As a customer, you need to be well versed in these plan options and understand the limitations and the service level guarantees.

THE FOUR DIALS

Choosing the right service and pricing mix for your organization is critical and can depend on the following things. These are what I call the "four dials" that you can turn to see which is the right solution for you.

The first dial is your current infrastructure environment. You need to know what it looks like. For example, if your PCs and your desktops are five-plus years old, you may require more support. If you're out of hardware warranty support on your systems, you may need a different level of service. If your systems are off-brand, what we used to call "white box," and aren't made and supported by a major manufacturer, you may have challenges.

If we walk into an office's server room and we see frayed and unlabeled cables, disarray and smoke, we will figure that the network is being held together with bale wire and bubblegum and needs to be stabilized.

The second dial is the level of your end user's technical sophistication. That's not an obvious attribute, and not a lot of people take it into consideration, but it's very important. We've supported organizations in the past that have teams of biotech-savvy PhDs doing cutting-edge gene research. Ironically, some of these people have needed more help learning how to use shared public calendars than, say, users of another one of our clients, a small, urban manufacturer located in a downtown area.

You can't simply choose by the level of experience of your user community. You and the provider really need to understand the issues that your employees are seeing, which, by the way, can be impacted by your current infrastructure environment that we just discussed. We need to understand the types of applications that are being run, the kind of data, and problems that you're seeing.

Businesses with better-trained employees should always have fewer technology problems than what we call the needy users. Neither are bad nor good...

The third dial is the number of employees and locations, including office locations. You need to know your total number. There are efficiencies (and lack of efficiencies) that come with different numbers of users, employees, or locations.

For example, if you have many remote locations with each staffed by two or three people, a certain approach to support will be required. It may not always be easy or possible to visit on-site for many small remote locations. You may need a remote-only, per-user, or per-device type of model.

As another option, if you have one office location with a highly dense environment, all of your employees on the same floor in the same office, and there are efficiencies built into supporting those users, you can use a uniform approach. You can have people on-site who can potentially address multiple problems, either concurrently or sequentially, right at the same location.

Knowing the employees' location, and whether they telecommute or are full time or part time, becomes another important element in figuring out the type of solution.

The fourth dial is the type of industry that the business serves or supports. A manufacturer will have certain needs versus a law firm versus a financial concern versus health care providers. It's another important factor for determining the right product mix.

TURNING THOSE DIALS

In short, the USE formula is a combined approach that recognizes clearly that one size does not fit all and also addresses the four different aspects of modern IT management needs. As we have seen, at least six pricing options have developed. Which is best for you? You can find out by setting those dials. Our ability to assist you in finding the answer is based on experience, judgment, and feedback from customers.

It's hard to just write a single prescription for a typical business. That is one of the big pitfalls of polarized IT support, in which the needle goes all the way to either the old or the new. We have customers that have come to us after spending a year or so under a fully managed remote price-fixed model, where they never met a technician face-to-face or were able to talk to someone besides the most junior help desk or PC technician on the phone. They came to us saying, "We want to be able to get the benefits but we don't want to be so far removed from knowing where our expert is." We have seen that boomerang effect.

Others tell us, "We've been stuck with one technician for several years and he's a great person, but he's not staying up in the forefront of technology. He's stale, and has gotten kind of lazy. We don't see any future in this. We're not getting recommendations to help us compete. And our prices are swinging wildly."

These are typical complaints. An expert can write the correct prescription, after asking the right questions and understanding the firm's particulars. When it comes to technology support, here's the bottom line: For many companies that can't afford their own IT department, a balanced approach, as with most things in life, tends to be the best course.

Traditional support is too weighted with risk, and fully managed "standoff" support is often too much of a cultural shock for employees who are used to seeing and knowing their own IT tech. Again, when no one from tech support shows up to your office holiday party, it's probably time to rethink your strategy, in my opinion.

It's all in the customer's hands. You can choose, and a competent professional can help you decide what works best for you.

ESSENTIALS OF THE USE APPROACH

When you research a hybrid support model, you should focus on three essential aspects.

FIXED FEE PRICING

First, you want your infrastructure managed for a fixed fee, regardless of the type of pricing approach that you ultimately get. Infrastructure means PCs, mobile devices, network devices, and servers. That is almost seen as commodity support today, because these systems are generally very stable and often at least partially fix themselves. The software and hardware advances in this area are tremendous.

So you want the infrastructure or what we call the "architecture" to be substantially or completely managed at a predictable price. That requires remote monitoring management, unlimited help desk access, tools, and technologies. The key is predictability. When you get your car's oil changed, you want to know it will be the same price every time. Oil is essential, and it's a service you must obtain, and you want to get that commodity at a known cost.

SCHEDULED ON-SITE SUPPORT

Scheduled on-site support is the notion that you have a technical consultant, with whom you may or may not be familiar, spend time at your office, "desk side," much like the traditional on-site model.

Scheduled support is predictable insofar as there are a certain number of repeat monthly hours that your technician will visit. It is a nod to the personalized approach of the traditional break/fix model. But this is different because that scheduled technician is not necessarily providing the same old traditional tasks. Those are covered by the first trench, which is the fixed pricing for unlimited infrastructure support that we discussed.

The technical consultant comes on-site and handles everything else. He tackles unresolved issues. He does some one-on-one training. He provides expert advice to upper management. He is a shoulder to lean on. The idea is to provide that level of comfort that is often needed in the technology world.

The one-two punch approach of unlimited infrastructure management coupled with a measure of on-site service provides that desired balance between the old and the new styles of service, and in my opinion is key to keeping customers happy over the long term.

YOUR VIRTUAL CIO

Let's take a closer look at the virtual chief information officer, the vCIO. A chief information officer of a company is ultimately responsible for your technology footing. He or she is responsible for making high-level architectural decisions on what technology the company will leverage to stay competitive.

Most small businesses cannot afford their own full-time CIO. So under the Dataprise USE framework, if you've purchased vCIO hours, you get a very high level, part-time CIO, which is generally all you need. What does the vCIO do? The vCIO analyzes your business needs, plots strategy, gives advice, and takes a seat at the executive table just as your full-time executive team would do.

The vCIO's job is twofold. First, it's to turn technology into a competitive advantage for your business, and to give you the expertise, advice, and high-level recommendations that a small business needs—to cloud or not to cloud, to use Application Suite A or B, how to look at big data, how to look at IT security concerns, and how to economize and leverage technology. It's very high level.

Second, the vCIO is the "program administrator" who's ultimately going to be responsible for making sure that your infrastructure management and your scheduled support staff ultimately do a great job. He or she is responsible for advisory services and high-level administration of the program itself.

At Dataprise, one of the key deliverables of our vCIOs is to provide an IT roadmap to the customer. This living and breathing document is updated at least annually and provides the options, budgets, and rationale for the business to pursue its technical goals over time.

ALL THE DIFFERENCE

These three components are the hybrid approach in different quantities and levels:

- Infrastructure management at a fixed price, whether it's environmental, per-user, or per-device.

- Some level of scheduled, on-site embedded visits from your trusted technician.

- Your high-level vCIO.

As a provider, flexibility is also key. We have clients who start out with a lot of on-site scheduled support and then over time back that down to almost nothing, and then they're left with a vCIO and unlimited infrastructure management. We've got clients that have a lot of vCIO but that have some internal technology resources, so they need minimal help desk from us and minimal scheduled support. Others require a lot of 24/7 infrastructure management and help desk, but they have their own high-level vCIO or CIO-type resources.

Those three additional components distinguish the service that we offer at Dataprise. It's important that you have a relationship with a managed services provider beyond the commoditized services—by which I mean the break/fix and infrastructure monitoring type of services.

Look at it this way: For an oil change, you can take your car to a low-cost shop, or to your car dealer. The dealership, however, will be offering you additional services. They're going to offer you a loaner car. They're going to offer you discounts on other types of services. They're going to treat you really well. They may even escort you to and from your place of business.

Similarly, everyone is going to offer their own brand of infrastructure management for some sort of fixed price. But the difference, in my opinion, is in the advice that you get, the personalized services that you receive, the comfort of your employees and your users, and the high-level touch of the vCIO. Put all together, A + B + C = a comprehensive solution, as is the case with the Dataprise USE approach.

DOWN TO THE
FINAL CHOICE

As IT management has evolved in the small to medium-sized business arena, we've gotten to a place where we understand that the middle of the road is usually the best path. The remaining question is what to look for in a managed services provider.

We've discussed how it's very important to look at the types of services that the provider is going to offer, particularly the hybrid. But there are a lot of providers. In the United States alone there are probably several thousand providers coast to coast. The typical size today of a successful MSP is generally fewer than 20 employees, with approximately 50 clients or so under management. But as I've hinted in this book, the MSP landscape is changing rapidly, just as the supported technologies and management models themselves are changing. Will the industry stay small and fragmented with lots of local MSPs, or will some big company swoop in and successfully offer an effective nationwide solution? It's still too early to tell, but my money is—that's right, you guessed it—right down the middle.

LIFE AFTER THE BIG BANG

That old Apple II that captivated me at age 13 was one of the machines that launched the personal computing revolution, even though you couldn't do much with it besides play some floppy disk–based games. We weren't connected then. The connected age of technology was still ahead of us.

I was a boy finding my own way, teaching myself, as did some of my peers and countless others who took these technologies and embraced them and discovered where they would fit. These modern technologies were created largely without a purpose and the purpose came later as people started to figure out how these things ought to be leveraged and used.

And then came the Big Bang. That was the effect that the Internet had on business technology. Business technology did, of course, predate the advent and the growth of the Internet. But the Internet explosion of the early 1990s was the spark that drove all types of businesses, big and small, into the next universe. That expansion and growth continues to this day. And that's really my message to you—technology is here to stay, and the pace of development if anything has picked up in the last few years. So don't go it alone—the risks are too great and the rewards missed could be even greater.

Today, not only is the IT industry so diverse, and not only is the barrier to entry so low, but the people with the skills are in huge demand for high-paying jobs. Those in the IT industry didn't experience the high unemployment rates that others faced during the recent recession. There has been a shortage of IT-capable people in business since the dawn of this modern age. It's a remarkable field in which someone in their early 20s, with little or no work experience, who is self-taught and competent with computers and networking (like I was), can today get a high-paying job. Typically, even entry-level IT professionals earn a minimum of about $40,000 per year. We have hired people for $50,000 or $60,000 a year with almost no experience but who are very capable and have high potential. In what other industry would that be the case?

However, unlike other knowledge-based professions, which require extensive schooling, exams, and credentials, there has not been a cry toward standardization and accreditation in the IT industry. There are several reasons for that.

One is that the evolution and the metamorphosis into high technology has happened so rapidly. Structural engineering has been around for centuries. The current wave of technology has been around for 30 or 40 years. IT is still really in its infancy.

The second reason is the wide disparity of what's out there. We have many manufacturers, many technologies, many developers and applications—and so many different ways to solve problems with technology that it is almost impossible to contain, measure, and harmonize it all.

At the same time, the cost of business technology is so cheap, relative to other types of industries, and so easily obtainable that any high school student can buy a PC and get a manual and some software and some tools and start tinkering from his or her home. As a result, many cottage industry companies have sprung up, increasing the innovation even more.

Those pioneers who heralded the computer age often felt obsolete by the time they retired—such was the pace of change in an era in which it seemed that a smart high school kid could run circles around someone with years of experience.

The expertise is diverse and unbridled, and the self-taught experts have outpaced university-level training and what the academic world has formalized. An example of that is web development. Although the Internet arose from university and governmental institutions, many of the innovations have come from individuals working out of their homes and in small businesses and cooperatives.

The standards have changed so much that academia has looked to the business world for guidance, in contrast to many traditional industries, where the academic world sets the par and the business community expands from there.

It is still like the Wild West in terms of accreditation and standardization. Most people know a neighborhood kid who probably could install your home Wi-Fi, computers, and Internet for just a few dollars. Likewise, they could sink a small fortune into someone with years of experience but who hasn't kept up the pace, and is lost amid the innovations.

To be self-taught is seen as sort of a badge of honor in the IT business. When hiring an IT professional, you may find someone who's very capable and entirely self-taught. Or you may find a former accountant who dabbled in IT and then obtained some IT certifications through vendor training classes. Or you might find an engineer who spent four years at an accredited engineering program or university after obtaining a bachelor's degree in, let's say, computer engineering.

HOW DO YOU SORT IT ALL OUT?

It leaves a small business wondering, "Where is the best place to turn?" The answer, in short, is that you need to hook up with a managed services provider on whom you can depend to help you sort it out.

However, you still might not know whom that provider will, well, provide. There's no way, as a small or medium-sized business, that you can really understand the different kinds of expertise that you're going to get. It's hard to tell, even from a resume, because of the lack of accreditation and standardization and training. This is beginning to change. There are initiatives under way, across the IT industry, to provide some accreditation and credentials to IT managed services providers and the people that work there.

An example of a provider-based certification is the SAS 70 standardization. SAS stands for Statement on Accounting Standards. SAS 70 is an accounting CPA-based audit that is geared toward service organizations of all types but particularly IT service organizations.

The SAS 70, and its recent successor, a similar audit known as the SSAE 16, have been popular in the financial and financial-related community. It has not seen widespread adoption across the IT sector, however, and there are reasons for this. It's very expensive for providers to obtain. The audits are not always performed in a uniform manner, and the goals established for service organizations are very complex and, frankly, beyond the reach of a lot of smaller IT service providers. And many consumers are still not widely aware of these things.

In addition, there's a relatively interesting new organization that's been around for a dozen or so years called "MSP Alliance." They're located at www.MSPAlliance.com, and they're an independent organization that only caters to managed services providers. They have started their own audit and accreditation program, directly targeted to the MSP community. The MSP Alliance organization strives to "promote cloud computing and the managed services industry as a true and viable profession, to the business consumer," and offers a certification tailored specifically toward MSPs. In 2014 my firm Dataprise underwent an MSP Alliance certification. I can report that the process was very thorough and we learned a lot about how to improve our operations to be more consistent. I recommend that all MSPs perform a similar review of their internal operations.

My point is that there are new initiatives under way. It's as if they're starting to tame the Wild West. It's as if the sheriff has come to Dodge to bring some order to town.

THE PROSPECT OF REGULATION

Why is accreditation important? Well, IT is not just a nice thing to have. It's something that organizations depend on, that could be critical to their mission and their very existence, and that could even be a matter of life and death. If technology fails at a hospital, for example, dire consequences can occur. If software or systems fail in a fly-by-wire airplane, hundreds could perish. Those are consequences that are not difficult to imagine in a real-time or critical system. If a civil engineer who builds safe bridges must be certified, you can see why certification would be important for those who develop and monitor the technology on which people's lives depend—whether it's the 911 emergency system, airplane software, or the many medical devices of the life sciences.

An issue here, however, is that IT accreditation is not government mandated. You would think that the government would, at some point, want to be involved in making sure that those types of technologies are built, supported, and maintained by certified engineers and certified professionals. I think we will be seeing more of that—as well as the industry interest, such as with the SAS 70, and SSAE 16, and now the MSP Alliance.

Now, the flip side of that is that people get worried that government involvement would stifle innovation and slow down progress, and that's sort of a double-edged sword. The technology is at the forefront of our progress and fuels our economy. It gives small business not just a competitive leg up locally but allows us to compete globally. I would be an advocate for perhaps some governmental regulation, but we want to be wary of onerous types of regulatory control.

The industry fights tooth and nail to avoid regulations. You read a lot about the government's role in net neutrality on the Internet, of making sure that the Internet and Internet providers stay neutral and available to everyone, and their efforts have repercussions across all facets of the industry. One of the negatives of government regulation in IT accreditation would be if it resulted in a very high bar of certification, accreditation, and training— to the point where we inhibited the ability for people to be self-taught and get into the industry quickly. That clearly would have a dampening effect on the flow of people into the talent pool.

Some of our international competitors, like the Chinese and others, are turning out computer scientists at 10 times the rate of this country. Until we can boast the same numbers, we need to be careful about clamping down on types of training and educational backgrounds required for technologists across the board.

Standardization and accreditation are starting to develop as they have in so many other industries and professions. We're still in the early stages.

THE BIG AND THE SMALL OF IT MANAGEMENT

An interesting development over the last couple of years has been a polarization in the IT managed services provider space. Whereas we used to have a very large small-provider component, a respectable midsized-provider component, and a substantial large-provider component, we seem to be losing the middle.

Now, because of the changing market and the way that the infrastructure services we've discussed have been commoditized, a lot of middle-tier players have either gotten a lot smaller and gone out of business, or small and medium providers have been gobbled up by very large companies that wish to get into the small to medium-sized business support space. As of this writing, we see that trend continuing.

So what does that leave? What does the future MSP community look like? There are still thousands of very small managed services providers coast-to-coast. A typical managed services provider is a company that has a local geography that they service. It could be a portion of New York City, such as Lower Manhattan. It could be Orange County in Southern California, or greater Chicago. The typical provider is currently still very locally based.

As I mentioned before, the typical managed services provider has fewer than 20 employees. The owner/operator is integral in the business. It typically has an average of 20 to 50 clients that it services and supports. That's the profile today of typical managed services providers across the country—very local, very small. They are small businesses supporting other small businesses.

On the other side of the spectrum, there are very large companies that are either in the business or trying to get into the business. They include computer manufacturers, carriers such as Comcast and Verizon Business and Time Warner Cable, digital copier manufacturers such as Ricoh and Konica Minolta, and others. They're trying to monetize or capitalize on their rich client base of small to medium-sized business customers that they support with network and IT services. Hosting providers such as Rackspace and others have also recently joined in, and Internet providers like EarthLink have joined the fray.

My point to this is that it's a very fragmented space. We have lots of small providers that have always been there and then some really big ones. And there's still a smattering of midsize and larger providers, like Dataprise. We're a midsize provider. The industry is quickly evolving and morphing. The business consumer needs to understand that when selecting a provider.

How do you choose the right one? Consider the kinds of services that you're going to receive. Does your provider have the ability to provide you the rich mix of services that you need as an evolving business? A challenge with a very small provider is that they're local and may not have the ability to support regional, national, or international types of customers.

Also, a small company with fewer than 20 employees may not have the expertise on staff to solve a lot of challenges that your user community may come up with. For example, they may have a lot of technology support expertise with desktops and mobile devices, but nothing with virtual servers and cloud technologies.

We always ask the question, "Where does the MSP go when the MSP has a question?" And consider as well that a small company may not have the ability to offer true 24/7 round-the-clock support. If it has only 15 employees, for example, would it really have a weekend crew or an after-hours crew?

THE BOTTOM LINE

Technology and technology support have been rapidly evolving for 25 years or so, particularly for small to medium-sized businesses. The support side of the equation has never moved faster than it has since around 2007. The dedicated or virtual IT function is considered an integral and necessary part of doing business, period.

Nothing moves as fast as technology. Being on the leading edge of IT can provide your business the competitive horsepower that it needs to succeed where others may fail. So it's an investment that, if done right, can pay a tremendous amount of dividends.

There have been, as we've discussed, at least two traditional ways of receiving IT services in the past for small businesses. There was always the sense of traditional IT support, which, in recent years, has been supplemented by fully managed support as a second option. But now there's a third, hybrid option, which we feel is the best overall solution available today for the reasons that I've presented.

As a business owner or executive decision maker, you should think of IT and the support for IT as one of your greatest assets and a valuable way to improve your bottom line. Once you have selected the right technology partner to help you sort through the many options, you can get back to the business of doing what you do best.